Our Lady of
Benoni

Our Lady of Benoni

ZAKES MDA

WITS UNIVERSITY PRESS

Wits University Press
1 Jan Smuts Avenue
Johannesburg
South Africa
www.witspress.co.za

First published 2012

ISBN: (print) 978-1-86814-567-6
ISBN: (epub) 978-1-86814-594-2

Edited by Pat Tucker
Cover design and page layout by Michelle Staples
Printed and bound by Creda Communications

Contents

Of Voices And Visions

A Satirical Staging of 'Revelations' and
Redemption in a New Play by Zakes Mda

Sarah Roberts[1]

Our Lady of Benoni teems with anecdotes and incidents, pulses
with desire and frustration, juxtaposes different cultural
norms and plays exuberantly with fantasies and truths that
cluster around the subject of virginity. Its tone is zany, its
subject matter serious.

Zakes Mda's satire is a kaleidoscopic display of the
extremes to which men and women are prepared to go to
preserve and value what is 'virginal'. Mda presents us with
the consequences of transgressing socially instilled norms in
sexual behaviour: that which is polluted is seen and judged
to be dangerous to the good health and purity of a group, a
society and its culture. He shows us how taboos, superstition,
custom and moral ethics construct a 'map' to live by in
order to maintain an acceptable reputation and avoid being
stigmatised. Mda also exposes the superstitions, customs and
beliefs about sexuality that guide our everyday behaviour.
His new play explores relations between knowledge and sex,
along with how these are symbolised in the way we speak,
write and think about the female body and sexual politics.

Mda's writing draws on his extensive experience as a
theatre-maker who is thoroughly familiar with crafting
a means of speaking to an audience through the multiple
resources of the medium of theatre. He uses the setting (place
and time), characterisation, dialogue and action in a manner

that is both playful and profoundly challenging and searching in its treatment of contemporary issues.

His writing also draws on a richly informed and subtle appreciation of multiple dramatic and literary traditions. *Our Lady of Benoni* fuses satirical elements derived from classical poetry with a modernist sensibility. Mda synthesises Brechtian and Absurdist features of theatricality (story-telling techniques and ways of developing characters) that allow us to appreciate the fictional quality of the story he is telling. But at the same time, this work is a profound exploration of what it means to operate in the real world, the social and politically charged landscape that defines post-apartheid South Africa.

Stylistically adventurous and unafraid to deviate from established practices, Mda is boldly confrontational in his handling of the ways in which he shows us how attitudes to power, superstition, ethics and sex are constructed. He demonstrates how both African and European value systems, ethical codes and mores have traditionally been forged from a male perspective and thus establish unequal power relations between the sexes. The play portrays the way male views of sexual relations and female sexuality establish norms, ideals and taboos. Through a multiple layering of stories and images he shows how gendered identity constructs the boundaries of what is sexually permissible and endorsed. To put it simply, there are different expectations of girls and boys, men and women in terms of the way they behave, and these differences are culturally learnt, either consciously or unconsciously. The obligations and custodianship of the woman's body and sexual desires are the focus of this play.

Our Lady of Benoni is a carnivalesque display of the relations among different forms of 'knowledge' embedded in social relationships where patterns of dominance and mastery are taken for granted. The stage action is complemented by ongoing offstage action about which we, the audience, are updated: it concerns the trial of a priest who has been charged with rape and who, however inappropriately, in the light of his actions, has garnered support from women because he endorses the re-introduction of virginity testing. This 'spiritual guide' is constantly referred to as the 'Right Reverend Comrade Chief my Leader'. The title fuses traditional spiritual authority with modern secular political terminology and invites us to recognise the absurdity of holding this man in such high esteem.

The role of heading a community seems to belong unquestioningly to a male authority figure. But Mda asks us to question this. The proliferation of powers granted to this male leader hints at the extremes (and potential abuse) of such powers. It also demands that we consider the dangers of unthinking acceptance, endorsement or support of any leader's actions and behaviour.

The title of Mda's play announces that the most cherished standards and beliefs (which we might regard as 'guiding principles to live by') are available for scrutiny and even ridicule. The first two words, *Our Lady,* invoke both the Catholic Madonna and her subsequent 'visitations' to Lourdes in France and to Portugal.[2] The rest of the title (*of Benoni*) locates us firmly amid the mine dumps and urban sprawl of a modern East Rand town.

Past and current associations with what Benoni has come to 'represent' are evoked. These cultural associations include a familiar film and television advertisement of the late twentieth century that relied on the unexpected juxtaposition of a sophisticated lifestyle with more everyday mundane reality. In the advert a sultry and glamorous young woman is asked 'Where did you have your first Campari?' The setting and tone anticipate an exotic or romantic response. The answer is subversive and undercuts what we see with what we hear. The one word answer is delivered in a decidedly South African, rather than an Italian, accent: 'Benoni'. What is implicitly global, or even European and specifically Italian, is proclaimed local.

The advertisement relied on a set of associations attached to fantasies of upwardly mobile living. This motif has subsequently been layered with further narratives of 'fairytale success' in the star status achieved by two more recent Benoni celebrities: Oscar winner Charlize Theron and Charlene Wittstock, her Serene Highness of Monaco.

The action of the play probes the relations between what we see and what we can know. Different ways of knowing, as a foundation for social conduct, are pitted against one another. On the one hand, belief, as an act of faith, is frequently founded on what has reportedly been seen and attested to by a privileged individual, rather than on personal witness.

On the other hand, the rational method of enquiry and of testing an hypothesis (by amassing arguments as evidence for interpretation) is another means of developing convictions and understanding. Both come under scrutiny and are offset by yet another means of negotiating what is real or illusionary: bodily or 'carnal' knowledge exists without need for words or symbols. But it, too, is not free from questions of ethics, morality and obligation and is, perhaps, even more strictly controlled and codified than any other form of knowing.

The play explicitly links the faculty of sight with knowledge and faith, as opposed to blindness and ignorance. Carefully preserved relics are produced with reverence and care. But the treasuring of relics is lampooned in action crafted around a decidedly stale slice of toast.

Our Lady of Benoni (one Francesca Zackey) is a figure we will never personally meet. She becomes the object of a pilgrimage, and access to her is regulated and enforced according to the strictest hours of business and professional consultation. Francesca instructs suppliants who come to her to look directly into the sun and when the character, Lord Stewart, complies and is subsequently blinded, she disclaims any responsibility, with the words 'It is out of my hands. People look at the sun at their own risk. I am not the sun'. We can anticipate a scam from the outset and our enjoyment depends on discovering how it is unmasked, along with being challenged by the consequences of unquestioning faith.

Structure and characters

Mda's focus is on entrenched patriarchal systems, with their beliefs, attitudes and behaviour, in relation to the value properties of female virginity and the complex symbolism attached to it. The loss of virginity in exchange for gratifying sexual pleasures entails the sacrificial exchange of innocence for experience. This is the fixed and stable point around which a medley of vignettes and scenes is arranged and developed.

Three very different men (Professor, Lord Stewart and The Seller of Laughter) represent aspects of a multicultural urban society. They inhabit a common world: they 'live in' (or operate from) an unnamed Johannesburg public park. Their daily routines are made up of physical excursions from this communal site along with symbolic departures from the spatio-temporal present as they share the stories of their past, with each other within their stage playground and with the audience. Their migrations in memory or in real action all circulate around the issue of virginity, its violation or preservation, its importance and definition, its mystique, capacity and value.

The interdependence of the three male figures (all living on the margins of society) is offset by the sharp distinctions among them in terms of cultural identity and personal history. Despite their indigent lifestyles and status each retains a vestige of authority, dignity and the sheer instinct or drive for self-preservation. The characters of the literate scholar (the Professor), the 'Aristocrat-fallen-from-Grace' (Lord Stewart) and the youthful trickster (the Seller of Laughter) provide Mda with a matrix of positions from which to create a series of lively exchanges in which bizarre allegiances are delicately balanced.

Professor is a lynchpin around which another triadic set of relations is established and it is through this that Mda approaches cultural perspectives of virginity that are not clearly signalled in his title but which are, nonetheless, perhaps more dominant and prevalent in rural South Africa than those of Catholicism and its converts. It is through these three figures that we are made aware of the consequences and effects of violating sexual mores.

MaDlomo, a mature municipal worker – the park cleaner, is a former virginity tester from the village of KwaVimba in KwaZulu-Natal. She is, as importantly, the mother of Bongi, raped when she was three months old by a man with AIDS. This incident has far-reaching consequences and resurfaces in the final scene of the play. MaDlomo's presence is the catalyst that forces Professor, who comes from the same village, to reveal his past and his relationship with Thabisile, the fifth and final character, introduced only in the second act.

Thabisile is announced as a 'strict traditional Zulu girl' to whom Professor was betrothed and with whom he performed culturally endorsed *ukusoma*, or intercrural sex,[3] prior to their marriage. Denounced, stigmatised and ostracised for not being a virgin (on the basis of the evidence of unstained bed sheets after their wedding night), Thabisile left her husband and a proportion of the lobola was demanded as a form of rebate for 'damaged goods'. The stigma of a tarnished reputation comes into focus through this aspect of the play.

Professor's obsession with multiple theories of virginity comes from engaging with assorted printed 'texts'. These include Vesalius discovering the hymen in 1544; the works of Hanne Blank, 'a virginity historian', and newspaper anecdotes with tantalising snippets of information. We may wonder initially whether these are genuine publications or fantastic fabrications, but Mda's method of working through careful research and reading around a serious subject is a clue that this is a topic that scholars have studied and journalists have pursued and we are required to consider how we process information that comes from such different sources. We are invited to recognise how theories and contemporary reportage, two different ways of considering a topic, appeal to our understanding on very different levels.

The game being played here is a serious one: the authority of printed material and the academic tradition is potentially deceptive and no less immune from satirical commentary than religious belief. Should we always believe what we read? Professor's self-appointed programme of learning about multiple approaches to what virginity represents is not an isolated study. He is intent on revealing the ways in which individuals and groups behave as a consequence of their beliefs: power, knowledge and language are bound together and jointly construct the world that we inhabit. The real effects on people's lives generated by the mythic 'truths' are his concern.

Text and performance

In 2002 Witwatersrand University Press published three plays by Zakes Mda: *Fools, Bells and the Habit of Eating*, with the significant subtitle, 'Three Satires'. This subtitle serves as an all-important framing device to guide the reader's reception and interpretation of the plays. In addition, the introduction, written by critic and director Rob Amato, contextualises the plays within the body of Mda's writing and work in the theatre, providing the reader with a sense of the early works from the period 1970–1990 and the plays written after the unbanning of the ANC on 2 February 1990.[4]

Readers are referred to this earlier anthology, firstly, because of the richness of the material it contains and secondly because Amato sets up a way of approaching Mda's particular style of theatre-making, on which this introduction expands.[5]

A private, solitary reading of a play differs from the process of the rehearsal room, with its commitment to joint discovery of ways in which the vitality, tonal contrasts, rhythmic patterns and variations proposed by the script materialise in words and images, sounds and silences, textures and colours as the dynamics of the action and its style, or idiom, take shape. As Amato puts it: 'This is not to say that the armchair director, the reader of the text, hasn't got plenty to think about and respond to, but that's harder than watching a developed "reading" on stage' (Mda 2002, p xvi). In his introduction Amato coins a new term, which he playfully defines in the style of an orthodox dictionary entry: 'Mdada (n), *also* Mdadaism: elusive black theatrical satire in the old and new Southern Africa' (2002, p v). He exploits the pun on Mda's name in a way that proclaims a particular status for Mda's work in terms of its genre, narrative mode and subject matter.

In Amato's words, 'Mdadaism' means 'truthful exaggeration' (2002, p vii), which integrates 'dream-based logic' with a more rational analysis of South African reality. The approach allows for a seamless fusion of the world of the imagined and magical or fantastical with the routine of everyday experience, without separating these two worlds into discrete categories or compartments.

The action of *Our Lady of Benoni* is located in a single, well-observed local setting: a Johannesburg public park in 2006, a public 'playground' containing a swing, a see-saw, a merry-go-round and a park bench – a location familiar to those who drive or walk around Johannesburg – and the story that unfolds is constructed around distinctly topical contemporary social issues or problems. These elements suggest the mode of realism that we are accustomed to on stage and in television drama. It would, however, be a profound mistake to approach the play anticipating that the drama will unfold by conforming to the conventions of realism. Like the 'well-made play', realism depends on sequential linear action clearly grounded in a logically connected sequence of probable events, which unfold to reveal complex, psychologically defined individual characters.

There is something liberating in what Mda does with this 'real' setting, which is, ultimately, only superficially familiar. Rather than focusing on a single personal narrative and correspondence with life as it is lived and experienced, drawing on observed detail and mirroring the world to which the action refers, Mda *fictionalises* the world in which he locates his theme. The park is a cultural playground and a stage for discussing ideas, rather than an environment that shapes and determines the identities of the characters.

His play-making strategies are directly at odds with

realism and celebrate the pleasures of the way stories are generated and transmitted with full consciousness on the part of the storytellers and actors. The sheer theatricality, entertainment value and humour of *Our Lady of Benoni* should not be underestimated. As Sheri Klein (2007, p 128) observes, 'the Latin root word for entertainment is "intertenere", which means "keeping in the midst". Art that is entertaining through its abilities to incite laughter enables us to be kept in the midst of the most current and pressing issues facing us on the planet.' Our certainties are debunked and our serious commitment to the 'business' of living is required to shift in perspective. The Seller of Laughter reminds us of precisely this proposition when he says 'Laughter is a goddamned serious business'.

Satire and stylised characters; medley and montage

The most rudimentary definition of satire (according to *Chambers English Dictionary*) is 'a literary composition, essentially a criticism of folly or vice, which it holds up to ridicule or scorn – its chief instruments [are] irony, sarcasm, invective, wit and humour'. From this perspective, satire is the antithesis of the 'praise poem', since social critique is an essential feature of the genre. Accordingly, satire, as Joseph T Shipley (1970) claims, 'deals less with people as such than with mental attitudes'.

While the genre of satire may be defined in broad terms there is also scope for identifying different forms or types of satire within this larger category. South African theatre from the mid-eighties onwards has opened up the space for appreciating the distinctions between the sharply observed, personally directed critique of key political figures and more generic castigation of unidentified representatives of the establishment.

Mda is not simply perpetuating a broadly defined tradition of satire: rather, he identifies distinctions between different forms of the genre. From this highly informed perspective he evolves an individual, hybridised and contemporary approach to satire within the Southern African context. In commenting on his intentions for this play, he writes: 'My play is meant to be a juxtaposition of Horatian and Juvenalian satire.' The declaration suggests just how formidably crafted and productive Mda's masterful play with satirical forms will prove to be.

Horatian satire is described by Shipley (1979, p 287) as being 'genial and general'. It tends to ridicule characters and mobilises 'the socially (as distinct from morally) corrective function of satire' (1979, p 287). Rudd (1973, p 11) makes a claim for Horace that guides an understanding of Mda's stance: 'His interests were focused entirely on man. Politics, then, were nonsense and religion didn't count.' Bearing this in mind with reference to the way Mda approaches the subject of virginity, we might argue that for Mda neither politics nor religion, institutionally founded or personally derived, will authorise or sanctify modes of behaviour that ultimately abuse power between individuals.

The comparison between the satiric modes of Horace and Juvenal provides a way of understanding what it is that Mda sets out to achieve and also hints at why he chooses to combine these disparate approaches. Rudd (1973, p 11) observes that 'whereas Juvenal works on the emotions by presenting a series of vivid pictures, Horace operates on the intellect by various rational procedures'.

Mda is unflinching and uncompromising in exposing the stark and brutal consequences of believing that sex with an innocent or pure (virginal) body − as in the rape of an under-age girl child − is an effective means by which a man may combat an HIV-positive status or AIDS. There are, quite simply, no grounds by which to legitimate or defend such beliefs: accommodating such abuse in any society is a sign of dangerous 'degeneracy' and frenzied desire that support the rights of an adult male at the expense of others. The shared history that binds Professor and MaDlomo will unfold to reveal the brutal and tragic consequences of perpetuating the myth that legitimates the violation and abuse of the most vulnerable subjects of this society.

Gail Fincham, in *Dance of Life* (2011, p 80) and, more specifically, in her analysis of Mda's novel, *The Madonna of Excelsior*, argues that 'Mda's explorations of refigured identity are rooted in his strong painterly imagination'. She proceeds to examine the link between the novel and the paintings of Frans Claerhout, which are so important to the story being told. The same intensely visual way of approaching storytelling on stage is evident from the way in which *Our Lady of Benoni* is written.

Imagining the play on stage offers us the chance to think of it as a series of unfolding tableaux, animated cartoon pictures as vivid and stark as Claerhout's paintings and as capable of triggering powerful emotional responses. It is this visual dimension of the play that moves us in ways different from intellectual analysis and from following the interplay of arguments and points of view expressed in the storytelling episodes.

Mda acknowledges the one-dimensional nature of the characters around whom the action is constructed. He writes:

'The characters are not round but flat [...] Satire by its very nature takes only one dimension of a character and then exaggerates it for the purpose of ridicul[e].'[6] The male characters are clearly conceived of as 'types'; their identities conform to their names and allow a patterned set of exchanges of ideas to take place. Stuart Hall (2003, p 257) quotes Dyer in defining 'types': 'a *type* is any simple, vivid, memorable, easily graspable widely recognised characterisation in which a few traits are foregrounded and change or "development" is kept to a minimum [emphasis in the original]'. *Our Lady of Benoni* leaves us in little doubt about the multiple ways in which value judgements are made and on what grounds. Social acceptability and integration within a collective are contrasted with being marked as deviant and 'excommunicated'. The boundary line of acceptability, as far as patriarchal views of female sexuality go, is an intact hymen – the guarantor of chastity – and its rupture is intricately bound up with the transfer of status and 'ownership' that accompanies orthodox marriage ceremonies.

Mda emphasises how his writing serves his critique of patriarchy:

> the characters are flat by DESIGN not by accident. They are flat because in a successful satire characters MUST be flat. Characters represent ideas and ideals rather than real flesh-and-blood people [...] that is why some of the motivations of the various characters may not seem rational to a person who is ignorant of how satire functions.[7]

Mda is not simply skirting the issue of why the characters lack depth and complexity or multi-dimensional psychological plausibility, he is addressing the necessary patterning that makes the play of ideas vivid and memorable.

To understand what a stylised character might be and how potently this may affect us as viewers, it is appropriate to look long and hard at Claerhout's paintings. The figures have their torsos and features outlined in a strong graphic line, their forms and features simplified and exaggerated.[8] Vivid colour, bold brushstrokes, exaggeration and emphasis may initially startle us if we compare these with a photograph, but the impact of these searing images will outlast the subtleties of detailed and exact reproduction of the specific and the actual.

Mda's vision ultimately embraces the capacity for healing and transformation. Thabisile's arrival in the park is the catalyst for a final reckoning on Professor's part. Violations that have previously been undeclared and long repressed are acknowledged. Mda shows us that responsibility and accountability for one's actions hold more redemptive potential than continued non-disclosure, denial and the attempt to remain isolated from kith and kin.

Reflecting on the play one becomes increasingly aware of how its structure depends on sharp contrasts and twists and the extent to which, in this fictional world, the inner logic of ideas overrides the demands of a plausible and probable unified plot founded on 'one deed that unwinds in all its entirety'.[9] The montage of disparate scenes fragments the action, as in a Brechtian epic, and as spectators and witnesses we are prompted to engage with positions being advanced and judge for ourselves what values and beliefs we may subscribe to.

The mixture and the medley are presented to us in order that we may engage and evaluate what is at stake. As spectators we are never placed in the position of an invisible voyeur seated in a dark auditorium, a silent witness to a private life being played out in public. In Mda's play private stories and intimacies are all but shouted out in public and fully displayed to the assembled gathering. The presentation of these interactions is openly declared as a construction for our delight and consideration. The line between performing a role on stage or playing a part in everyday life in order to uphold what is expected of who we are, is very fine: the boundaries between art and life are blurred as we recognise how in our everyday lives we too construct stories about ourselves and beliefs and play out our parts.

'Mdadaism'

In conclusion, as a means of reconsidering Mda's use of satire I turn to Dada and its principles, operation and the responses it elicits. Richard Sheppard (2000, p 197) explains that Dada can be understood on three levels:

> [1] it names an amorphous Bohemian movement
> [2] it characterises a complex of existential attitudes, which while varying from person to person, are vitalist and involve the achievement of balance amid fluctuating opposites. But at the third level, it is used by some of the Dadaists to name a life force that is simultaneously material, erotic and spiritual, creative and destructive.[10]

It is this third sense of the term that most concerns us in approaching Mda's theatre, with its affirmation of lives that improvise so energetically; with a spirit that admits no defeat and ultimately seeks out dignity in assorted strategies of survival in the flux and mayhem of life through relationships and the sense of community. Critics of Dada reject its anarchic impulses in terms of political creed, its 'childishness' and/or 'nihilism' and (at the other end of the spectrum) accuse Dadaists of elitism (Sheppard 2000, p 171).

In Sheppard's view these attitudes ignore the most important attribute of Dada, which is that it 'involved one of the first major attempts to bridge or even abolish the gap between "high" élitest art and "low" popular literature' (Sheppard 2000, p 171). It may be that Mda's achievement is to accomplish just this. He draws on, and synthesises, the idiom of orality with the conventions of literary tradition; with the chains that link the Seller of Laughter to Lord Stewart he binds together street savvy and knowledge that derives from a different order; the intellectual operations of the mind are fused with the erotic; the boundaries between oppressor and victim, dominant and subjugated forces, are dismantled.

Contemporary South Africa, as in 2006, remains a society in transition, embroiled in some respects in the process of socio-political changes of significant magnitude and, in other respects, equally trapped in a stasis that reproduces past inequalities. Everyday social encounters are fraught with tensions between preserving (and re-inventing) tradition and modernity, privilege and poverty.

Mda seems to invite us to recognise that 'unpredictable energies' are potentially restorative. Fittingly, the last word of the play goes to the resourceful Seller of Laughter, whose 'final solution' to his own creative problem and Lord Stewart's dilemma is a triumphant defence of humour and performance, and ultimately of the genre of satire itself.

'Mdadaism' celebrates the generative capacity of the human spirit and consciousness and lays great store in our capacity to talk to each other, to listen to each other, and, through these encounters, we can begin to unsettle the heritage of authority and the abuse of power. By recognising absurdities we can affirm the dignity and value of the individual and the society and the interdependent relationship between the two.

Notes

1   Sarah Roberts has worked in theatre for the past 33 years designing sets and costumes for a variety of directors and choreographers. She is currently Skye Chair at the Wits School of Arts where she lectures in the Drama Division.

2   The peasant girl, Bernadette Soubirous claimed that in 1858, at the age of 14, she saw the Virgin Mary in the village of Lourdes. She further claimed that the Virgin had granted the spring waters of the grotto of Lourdes healing powers and it has become a site for pilgrims seeking cures for a wide range of illnesses and disabilities. Our Lady of Fatima is the title bestowed on the Virgin Mary who is said to have appeared to three shepherd children in Portugal, in 1917.

3   This is explained to Lord Stewart in the course of the play as sex without penetration.

4   Mda's own 1990 essay about his early theatre work can be accessed in 'Maratoli Travelling Theatre: Towards an alternative perspective of development', contained in the *Journal of Southern African Studies* 16 (2), June, and in Gunner 1994.

5   Mda is also a prolific and celebrated novelist. His novels include *She Plays with the Darkness* (1995), *Ways of Dying*

(1995), *The Heart of Redness* (2000), *The Madonna of Excelsior* (2002), *The Whale Caller* (2005), *Cion* (2007) and *Black Diamond* (2009).

6   Unpublished correspondence, 16 December 2011.

7   Unpublished correspondence, 16 December 2011.

8   For example, *Women Harvesting, Profound Nostalgia, The Blue Madonna* and the *Musician* series. Mda's own painting of intertwined figures (Fincham 2011, plate XVI) also shows just how expressive two-dimensional painterly figures can be.

9   The phrase was coined by Emile Zola, the nineteenth-century French critic and writer, champion of the emergent phase of what was known then as naturalism, which corresponds to a contemporary understanding of realism.

10 Sheppard (2000, p 173) writes that 'Dada began in a fairly haphazard way in Zurich 1916, invented itself as it went along, and acquired an increasingly complex sense of itself over a period of years'. He stresses that it did not exist as an 'abstract set of rules and responses' and that it encompassed a wide range of responses to the sense of crisis and 'outrage at the unprecedented senseless slaughter of the Great War'.

Bibliography

Fincham, G. 2011. *The Dance of Life*. Cape Town: UCT Press.

Gunner L. 1994. *Politics and Performance: Theatre, Poetry and Song in Southern Africa*. Johannesburg: Witwatersrand University Press.

Hall, S. 2003. *Representation: Cultural Representations and Signifying Practices*. London: SAGE.

Klein, S. 2007. *Art and Laughter*. London: Tauris.

Mda, Z. 1990. 'Maratoli Travelling Theatre: Towards an alternative perspective of development'. *Journal of Southern Theatre Studies* 16(2):352–358.

—. 2002. *Fools, Bells and the Habit of Eating*. Johannesburg: Wits University Press.

Rudd, N. 1973. *The Satires of Horace and Persius*. Harmonds-worth, England: Penguin.

Sheppard, R. 2000. *Modernism-Dada-Postmodernism*. Evanston, Illinois: Northwestern University Press.

Shipley, J. 1979. *Dictionary of World Literary Terms*. London: George Allen & Unwin.

MDA ON MDA

Zakes Mda answers some questions about
Our Lady of Benoni

Interview with Pat Tucker

What prompted you to write the play?

Three events on separate occasions struck me as worthy of plays. First there were the black and white beggars that I saw among the mostly black vendors at traffic lights in Johannesburg. Some of the urchin beggars carried signs with lame jokes; that's what they were selling. I was fascinated by the whole scenario and I vowed that one day I would write a play about it. Then one day I read a newspaper report about Francesca Zackey in Benoni and her visions of the Virgin Mary. Many people believed her and made pilgrimages to her home – hence the title of the play, *Our Lady of Benoni*. You will remember that there is a long history of young girls seeing visions of the Virgin Mary. There are many sites the world over, especially in Europe, where this has happened. The best known among them are Lourdes and Fatima. The Virgin Mary is always referred to in relation to a particular site, depending on the context; for instance, Our Lady of Fatima and Our Lady of Lourdes. That is why we have *Our Lady of Benoni*. I decided that one day I would write a play about Francesca Zackey and filed the newspaper clippings recording her story.

On another occasion, years later, I read a fascinating book titled *Virgin: The Untouched History* by Hanne Blank (New York: Bloomsbury 2007). Blank has written a history of virginity and what it has come to mean in various cultures of the world. It was from this book that I learnt that some of the beliefs about virginity that we claim as African actually originated in Europe. Even virgin cures – such as the belief in some of the unenlightened corners of South Africa that having sex with a virgin cures AIDS – originate in Europe. The book is meticulously researched, with well-sourced case studies. This was an idea for another play.

In 2010 I was a writer-in-residence at Northwestern University in Evanston, near Chicago. That's where I decided to write one of these three plays. Then another idea struck me. Why three plays? The beggars, Zackey and virginity could all come together in a single play about the perils of virginity. That's how *Our Lady of Benoni* was born.

What was it about Francesca Zackey that made you choose her as the kick-off point for the play and, most importantly, the title?

I am always enthralled by stubborn faith. As a humanist and secularist I am always in search of evidence, despite myself. I therefore respect people who can plan their lives only on the basis of faith. I have always been fascinated by religious iconography and the mysteries of belief. I write about that in one of my novels, *The Heart of Redness*, which is about the prophecies of Nongqawuse, the teenage prophetess, who in 1857 claimed to have received a prophecy from the spirits of the ancestors which required the Xhosa people to destroy their cattle and burn their crops. I saw Francesca Zackey as continuing in the same tradition – young girls seeing visions and garnering large followings of the faithful. You will note that in the play, as in the novel, and also in another of my plays, *The Nun's Romantic Story*, I make no value judgement about faith and belief. I merely note its power – a person can stare at the sun, lose his sight and continue to believe. This actually happened in Benoni to one of the pilgrims. I make it happen to one of my characters in the play.

How did you choose the setting?

The park has always been my favorite setting. I wrote an earlier play, *We Shall Sing for the Fatherland*, set in a park. And here, since I was writing about a bunch of homeless people, a suburban park seemed an ideal setting.

How did you conceive and name the characters?

The characters themselves – who they are, what they believe, what others see in them – suggested the names to me. The characters, therefore, named themselves.

You have painted a fascinating portrait of the inner life of people most of us would write off as merely vagrants or 'the homeless'. How did you research your characters?

By mere observation. Artists are sensitive to many things that ordinary people take for granted. Although it was never my mission to do this, I observe that most of my work is set among the downtrodden and marginalised. I see humanity and compassion in and among them.

Your play has a strongly feminist theme. Do you hope that, through this play, members of your audience will be prompted to rethink their attitudes to women, girl children and the myth of the cure for AIDS?

I didn't know that I was a feminist because I never set out to be a feminist. It would be presumptuous and patronising of me to think I can speak for women. It would be an extension of the patriarchy that I deplore. But I have been called a feminist before. My first novel, *Ways of Dying,* was rejected by a famous publisher who called it a 'feminist diatribe'. I was surprised to hear that, because feminism was the furthest thing from my mind when I wrote the book. I was merely writing about life as I saw it. Perhaps my feminist sensibilities emerged in the process. There is a slogan that has become a cliché now: feminism is the radical notion that women are people too. It is true. I am appalled by cultural practices that violate women and girls, such as virginity testing, which King Shaka, in his wisdom, abolished two centuries ago, but which has now been revived in some reactionary reclamation of 'culture'. It is that very patriarchal 'culture' that has oppressed women, poisoned their bodies, and murdered them. Yes, I hope that audiences and readers will re-think their attitudes.

You present us with two women with apparently diametrically opposed views on the role and rights of women. On the one hand we have MaDlomo – very complex – feisty and independent but determinedly anti-feminist, with her commitment to virginity testing and her support of the alleged rapist. On the other we have Thabisile, from the same village and equally feisty and independent, but who has moved far from her traditional roots. Was your intention deliberately to contrast them?

Oh, yes, contrasts work effectively in storytelling! It is also important that your heroes should have flaws and your villains should have redeeming features. It is the only way your characters will have credibility. Even in a satire, where the essential flatness of your characters is by design, they still need to be credible.

Glossary

Adle kuphi umelusi? (isiZulu)
Where should the shepherd eat?

Ag shame! (Township slang)
What a pity!

Amadlozi (isiZulu)
Ancestors

Amampunge (isiZulu)
Crap

Angiyihlalel'imibhedo ke mina (isiZulu)
I'm not staying here for your nonsense

Angizidli izinkowankowane namakhowe mina (isiZulu)
I do not eat mushrooms

Aniz'thandi (isiZulu)
You don't love yourselves

Ausi (Sesotho)
Sister

Awuhloniphi wena (isiZulu)
You have no respect

Ayingeni ndawo la (isiZulu)
Has no place here

Badimo (Sesotho)
Ancestors

Bayethe, wena weZulu (isiZulu)
Ceremonial salute to the Zulu King

Chaaa! Weeee! (isiZulu)
Oh, no!

Cha ke manje (isiZulu)
Now you are

Cha ke manje ningohlule! Yiyo kanti into oyihlalele la eGoli?
Ukugonana nabelungu? (isiZulu)

Now I have seen everything! Is that what you're staying for here in Johannesburg? Hugging each other with white people?

Cha ngiyabona ke manje, ukuhlala nabelungu (isiZulu)

Now I can see that staying with white people

Foreisetata (Sesotho, from Afrikaans)

Free State

Futhi ke (isiZulu)

And another thing (or again)

Ha ke malala-phayiphu (Sesotho and township slang)

I am not a homeless person who sleeps rough

Ha ke sebeletsi mahala nna (Sesotho)

I don't work for nothing

Hamba gwala ndini! (isiZulu)

Go away, you coward!

Hau, mme (Sesotho)

Oh, mother

Hawu, kade bengizingene ngani izindaba zabantu? (isiZulu)

Anyway, why do I bother myself with other people's business?

Hawu, kanti (isiZulu)

Hey, so

Hayibo! (isiZulu)

Oh, no!

Ihlazo (isiZulu)

Shame

Ikhalela isinkwa namaSimba (isiZulu)

Is crying for bread and Simba chips

Imbhawula (isiZulu)

Brazier

Imihlolo! (isiZulu)

Wonders!

Intanga zakho (isiZulu)
People of your age

Iseqamgwaqo (isiZulu)
A 'loose' woman or prostitute

Isicholo (isiZulu)
Zulu traditional headdress for women

Isidwaba (isiZulu
Zulu traditional skirt

Isifebe (isiZulu)
A whore

Isilo samaBandla (isiZulu)
Praise name of the Zulu King

Izinto ozikhulumayo zingavala umuntu izindlebe (isiZulu)
The things you say can make one deaf

Kade ekudelela (isiZulu)
He has looked down on you

Kade ng'cabanga ukuth' ukhuluma ngomuntu (isiZulu)
obhadlile (isiXhosa)
I thought she was talking of a sane person

Ke moshan'a Foreyisetata kwana (Sesotho)
I'm a boy from the Free State

Ke tla u fumana ka leleng la matsatsi (Sesotho)
I'll get even one of these days

Klaar (Afrikaans)
Finished

Kwana (Sesotho)
Over there; yonder

Larney (also Lahnie) (Township slang)
White person; also someone who is well off

Le masepa kaofela (Sesotho)
You're all full of crap

Lento yenu ye-virginity (isiZulu and English)
This virginity matter

Lobola (Nguni)
Bridewealth
Manga (isiZulu)
Lies
Manga-manga (isiZulu)
hocus-pocus
Mayif'iBitch, if'iBitch! Bulal'iBitch, if'iBitch! (isiZulu and English)
Let the bitch die, kill the bitch, let the bitch die!
Mlungu
White man
Mme (Sesotho)
Mother, madam
Na kanti (isiZulu)
No English equivalent; phrase used to emphasise a question
Ngabelungu abanjani laba? (isiZulu)
What kind of white people are these?
Ngamla (Township slang)
Rich person
Ngisebenzel'izingane zami mina la kwa-maspala (isiZulu)
I'm working for my children here at the municipality
Ngiyabona ke manje ukuthi nihlala nabelungu la eGoli (isiZulu)
I see that here in Johannesburg you live with white people now
Ngiyahamba mina (isiZulu)
I am going (leaving)
Nguwe lona? (isiZulu)
Is this you?
Nguwe lo osho nje? (isiZulu)
Are you the one saying this?
Nkulunkuln wami
Oh, my God!

Ntate (Sesotho)

Father; sir; mister

ooMaDlomo (isiZulu)

MaDlomo and others

Oqambh'amanga ngaye (isiZulu)

Who lied about him

Phela ngumkhay'uMaDlomo (isiZulu)

Remember we are from the same village as MaDlomo

Phela wena (isiZulu)

Of course you

Rametlai (Sesotho)

Comedian; clown; joker

Re ntse re bapala (Sesotho)

We're still playing

Sinobuntu (isiZulu)

We have humanity

Suka! (isiZulu)

Go away!

Thebe e sehelwa hodim'a engwe (Sesotho proverb)

A new shield is stencilled from an older shield

Toyi-toyi (Township slang)

Protest dance

uBaba uMadonsela

Mr Madonsela

Ubheda ngani manje umlungu (isiZulu)

What is this white man dreaming about

uBongi wami (isiZulu)

My Bongi

Ubuntu

Humanity; humanness; personhood

Ucabang'ukuthi angizazi izindaba zakho wena? (isiZulu)

Do you think I don't know about your affairs?

Ukusoma (isiZulu)
Intercrural sex
U lelofa jwale monna kea u bona (Sesotho)
I can see that you're now a loafer, man
U-maid ngunyoko (English and isiZulu)
A maid is your mother
uMaria uhlangana kuphi nesinkwa? (isiZulu)
How does he connect Mary with bread?
Umelusi udla emhlambini (isiZulu)
A shepherd eats from his own flock
Umlungu wakho (isiZulu)
Your white man
Umthombo (isiZulu)
Sorghum sprouts used for brewing beer
Uthi ngiyi-poes? (isiZulu and Afrikaans)
You say I am a woman's genitalia?
Uyabona ke (isiZulu)
Do you see
Uyabona ke manje lapho (isiZulu)
Now you see there
Uyakuphi kanti manje? (isiZulu)
Where are you going now?
Uyamkhumbula mos uBab'uMkhonza? (isiZulu)
You do remember Mr Mkhonza, don't you?
Uze waziwa nayizingane (isiZulu)
Even children know you
Wang'thuka ke manje umlungu (isiZulu)
Now the white man is insulting me
Wathint'abafazi (isiZulu)
You touch (strike) a woman
Wena (isiZulu)
You

Wena ka lo (Fanagalo)
You are

Wena Sathane ndini (isiZulu)
You devil you

Wenza ukuthi angidelele mos (isiZulu)
You make him look down on me

Wenziwa yilabelungu ohlala nabo (isiZulu)
It is the fault of these white people you live with

Wubuntu bethu (isiZulu)
It is our humanity

Yho! Wangihlek'umlungu! (isiZulu)
Oh, the white person is laughing at me!

Yini ngawe kanti? (isiZulu)
What is wrong with you?

Yini uqamb'amanga ngami manje? (isiZulu)
Why do you lie about me now?

Yiqiniso ke lelo (isiZulu)
That is the truth

Yizingane zabantu lezi (isiZulu)
These are other people's children

Our Lady of
Benoni

Cast

PROFESSOR ... A black man in his mid-thirties. Quite clean and well groomed, despite the fact that his clothes are worn.

LORD STEWART ... An ageing white English-speaking South African with an affected British accent. Sometimes he forgets and slips into his South African accent. He looks like the hobo he is, although he tries to keep up appearances.

THE SELLER OF LAUGHTER ... A black street boy in his mid-teens. He tries very hard to be true to his name.

THABISILE ... A beautiful black woman, perhaps in her thirties. Was once betrothed to Professor.

MADLOMO ... A black woman park cleaner, usually dressed in an orange overall. A former virginity tester, she is quite assertive and obstinate, but is also compassionate.

THE TIME
Autumn 2006

THE SETTING
A park in a Johannesburg suburb

Act One

Scene 1

Lights come up on PROFESSOR, who is sitting on a bench reading a newspaper aloud. There is a pile of newspapers beside him and two or three books. The park is well kept and clean. The grass is green and there are flowers a few feet from the bench. LORD STEWART is sitting on a swing, which sways gently. He is eating a boerewors roll as he listens intently to the news as rendered by PROFESSOR. There are a merry-go-round, a slide and a see-saw nearby. All the playground equipment is in poor condition and exhausted, but not broken. It is still very functional. The swing squeaks to the rhythm of the swaying.

PROFESSOR [*reading*]: 'Thousands of people – yesterday
    I counted more than five hundred – flocked to the
    humble home in Tassenberg Road, Benoni, to receive
    blessings from Francesca Zackey, the South African
    teenager from a local Lebanese community.'

STEWART: Project! I can't hear you.

PROFESSOR: It's Nongqawuse all over again.

STEWART: What is?

PROFESSOR: Teenage girls making prophecies.

STEWART: Read louder.

PROFESSOR: You would hear me if you stopped that damnable

3

swing. It gets on my nerves, you know that. Maybe that's why you do it all the time, to get on my damn nerves.

STEWART: Why would I bother with your nerves, Professor? It is the only way I can relax after standing all day at the traffic lights. You should try it too sometime.

PROFESSOR: I hate that swing.

STEWART: I mean earning a living at the traffic lights. I don't know how you can afford to sit here all day long reading books and papers while we sweat in the hot sun. And so they say this lady has seen the Virgin herself?

PROFESSOR: Yeah! She was sitting with her mama and papa eating a dinner of spaghetti and meatballs when she was suddenly attacked by the scent of roses.

STEWART: We need roses here as well. Not just Easter flowers and whatever those purple ones are. I think they plant those because they are hardy. But they don't have any decent scent at all.

PROFESSOR: You're not paying attention, Lord Stewart. There were no roses there ... at the dinner table ... but the teenage girl could smell them. After dinner she went to her room and there, seated on her bed, was the Virgin Mary, Mother of Jesus.

LORD STEWART stops the swing and makes the sign of the cross. PROFESSOR looks at him, shakes his head and reads once more from the newspaper.

PROFESSOR [*reading loudly*]: 'Francesca said that Jesus's mother was very fair skinned, with brown hair and ice-blue eyes. She was wearing a royal blue veil and light was coming from her hands, the teenager said.'

Whoa! She doesn't look like anyone from the Middle East. The mother of Jesus is Caucasian!

STEWART: The teenager accused the Virgin Mary of not looking like someone from the Middle East?

PROFESSOR: No. It's me who is saying it. I didn't expect her to be some ditzy blue-eyed blonde.

LORD STEWART jumps down from the swing to join PROFESSOR.

STEWART: Brunette.

PROFESSOR: Brunette, blonde, same Caucasian difference.

STEWART: You just had to be racist about it. That's what the post-apartheid post-racial South Africa is all about. Always the race card.

PROFESSOR: I didn't invent the race card, Lord Stewart. When I was born it was there already, and it was being played against me by the white people.

STEWART: What paper is that?

PROFESSOR: The *Sunday Independent*. Why?

STEWART: Just to make sure it's broadsheet not tabloid. It's not that one that always has stories about tikoloshes and zombies and all sorts of Northern Province witchcraft? This is for real, is it?

PROFESSOR: I only read the news. I don't pass judgement. [*He continues to read.*] 'The Virgin Mary appeared to Francesca throughout the night, both inside the house and outside, in the yard. Francesca has placed flowers and candles at each spot where the Virgin Mary appeared. She said that "Our Lady" told her to pray the rosary and to get others to pray it, as though it was the last day on earth.'

STEWART: So, thousands flock to old Benoni to be healed by the Virgin? Francesca must be a virgin herself.

PROFESSOR: How do you come to that conclusion, Lord Stewart?

STEWART: Precedent, my dear fellow. Only virgins can see the Virgin.

The SELLER OF LAUGHTER bursts in, full of energy and hyperactivity. He is holding two flat cardboard signs high.

SELLER [*yelling excitedly*]: I've got a new one! I've got a new one! And this one is a killer, my man. I tell you, Lord Stewart, this one is going to kill them with laughter!

PROFESSOR: We're talking about something serious here.

SELLER: What's more serious than laughter? Laughter is a goddamned serious business!

He reaches for the merry-go-round, pushes it at full speed and jumps on it. The merry-go-round gains momentum and he breaks into laughter. He lifts his arms in an expression of joy. The laughter becomes more raucous as the merry-go-round goes faster. Then it begins to slow down, going slower and slower until it stops. He seems dizzy as he steps down and staggers to his boards.

STEWART: He must be high on his mushrooms.

PROFESSOR: Those mushrooms will kill him.

SELLER: They may call you Professor but your books haven't taught you a damn thing about zoomers.

STEWART: You call them zoomers?

SELLER: I didn't name them. That's what magic mushrooms

are called. Zoomers or shrooms. And they don't kill
anybody, for your information. They only give power,
love and happiness. They make me see beautiful
colours in the sky. They make me talk to my ancestors
– the Great Badimo. They give me inspiration to create.
And I need lots and lots of it. I am halfway there
already; I am going to compose the greatest joke ever.

STEWART: The Mother of All Jokes! And when the motorists
read it at the traffic lights it will brighten their day and
they will give you oodles of money.

He gives the SELLER OF LAUGHTER a high five.

SELLER: You are the man, Lord Stewart. You know what life
is all about. Unlike this one they call the Professor you
have worked the traffic lights and you know what the
deal is. Gone are the days when you could wear dark
glasses and stand there with a sign, 'Please Help the
Blind', and come back loaded with cash. The ngamlas
are wise to that trick now. They ignore your ordinary
begging signs about joblessness and kids to feed. They
want to laugh. And that's what I sell them. That's why
I am known far and wide throughout traffic-light-land
as the Seller of Laughter. Oh, yes! Even back in my
township, kwana Foreisetata, ntate, they called me
Rametlai.

PROFESSOR [*dismissively*]: Lord Stewart makes a lot of money
too, without holding up signs with lame jokes: 'Are
You Going to Give Me Money or Should I Fake a Limp'.
Or that common one that I have seen at every traffic
light: 'My Cat Arrested for Eating Neighbour's Chicken.
Please Help Me with Condolenss and Bail'.

SELLER: You can laugh all you want; those jokes have made
money for their creators, my friend.

7

STEWART: And for many other people who have plagiarised them and are using them for their own benefit.

SELLER: That is why the joke I am in the process of composing ... the greatest joke of all ... will be copyrighted. It's not going to be a commonplace one like cats eating chickens or faking limps. Nobody's going to steal my ideas. The Mother of All Jokes will be franchised. No one will use my joke without paying for it.

PROFESSOR: Even your friend and protégé, Lord Stewart?

STEWART: I don't need jokes to sell. I just stand there and look at them straight in the eye. Everyone has something to sell at the traffic lights: hangers, garbage bags, flowers, newspapers, even jokes. I have nothing to sell but my whiteness.

SELLER: You are not white, Lord Stewart. You used to be white, but not anymore. The sun has done its business on you.

STEWART: I don't need anything to sell because I've my whiteness. They give you more money when you're white.

SELLER: Look at you, man, no one can tell the difference between us anymore.

STEWART: Whites give you more when you're white. They see themselves in you and it scares the crap out of them. So they fill your bowl with gleaming coins. Blacks give you oodles of money too; it boosts their ego to be charitable to a white man. So, as a white beggar you win all round. When I was with Danni ... [*Sadly.*] They gave us more money when I was still with Danni ... when she stood there like a princess at the traffic lights. A beautiful, sun-drenched princess.

PROFESSOR: There's sadness in you every time you mention
  Danni. And yet you never want to talk about her.

*It is obvious that LORD STEWART doesn't want to talk about
Danni. Instead he goes to the pieces of cardboard lying on the
ground and tries to reach for them.*

STEWART: When are you going to unveil your new joke, O
  Seller of Laughter?

SELLER: No, give me back my signs.

STEWART: Come on, man, we are your comrades. We want to
  see the Mother of All Jokes.

*LORD STEWART runs away with the boards and the SELLER
OF LAUGHTER chases him among the playground equipment.
STEWART is too old to outrun the SELLER. So he throws the
boards to PROFESSOR, who continues the relay. When the
boards are with PROFESSOR the SELLER does not want to
continue the chase. It is clear that he does not like PROFESSOR
and does want to be part of any game with him. So he just
stands there and yells.*

SELLER: Give me my signs, you bastards!

PROFESSOR: Bastards? Awuhloniphi wena. Here!

He throws the boards at him. SELLER lets them fall on the grass.

STEWART: What's the big secret, anyway?

SELLER: You are the last one who should ask me that
  question, Lord Stewart. You know how it is out there at
  the traffic lights. I don't want anyone to see this yet. I
  still have to fine-tune it. I don't want anybody to steal it
  before I exercise my copyright on it.

PROFESSOR: Bah! Copyright! How do you exercise copyright
  on something scribbled on cardboard?

SELLER: They call you Professor and you don't know about copyright?

PROFESSOR [*laughs mockingly*]: Laugh all you want. This one is going to break all records.

STEWART: How does a joke break records?

SELLER: The one that's going to make me millions. The one that's going to make me be counted in the ranks of BEE Fat Cats. I'll be blasting you with exhaust fumes from my Rolls-Royce at the traffic lights. And don't you dare pretend you know me then.

He is fed up with them. He exits.

STEWART: He hates you.

PROFESSOR: Just a little resentment. Because I read newspapers instead of sleeping in them. That's what he told me once.

STEWART: He's jealous because you don't work the streets like the rest of us. Yet you live so well.

PROFESSOR: Live so well? In the park?

STEWART: I am jealous, too. It's just that I know how to hide it; he doesn't. You don't want for anything.

PROFESSOR: You don't know that, Lord Stewart. You don't know that. I am a tortured man. My soul is suffering. I am in my own hell. I look at you and him coming and going without any cares in the world and I am jealous.

STEWART: You don't beg like some of us have to.

PROFESSOR: Only because I hate the smug look of the giver. The giver is very selfish.

STEWART: These folks give us money because they are selfish?

PROFESSOR: You think they are altruistic? Maybe they are. But at the end of it all altruism is a selfish act. The selfish gene will always be there in humans. Altruism comes back to the giver because it makes him feel good about himself. It makes the giver happy to see someone happy as a result of his actions. I am not going to make any of these rich bastards happy at my expense.

STEWART: You can afford to say that because you are a man of independent means. And your means are secret because you are just as selfish as the givers you're talking about.

PROFESSOR: I share generously with all of you.

STEWART: Precisely. You are well heeled; the Seller of Laughter can see through the selfishness of your philanthropy.

PROFESSOR, caught in the trap of his own logic, laughs.

PROFESSOR: I am just as selfish to the Seller of Laughter too so he has no reason to hate me.

STEWART: Yes, sometimes when it rains and we're not able to go to the office ...

PROFESSOR: Office?

STEWART: Otherwise known as the traffic lights.

PROFESSOR: Oh, that's what you call it these days!

STEWART: When we can't go to work you do come to our rescue by donating something for our upkeep.

PROFESSOR: Or when winter nights are too vicious

even for imbhawula, I sacrifice my rands for your accommodation at the homeless shelters.

STEWART: That's all the more reason to hate you, the same way that you resent the bastards who give us money at the traffic lights for their smug charity. Another thing, of course, is that he thinks you despise him because he doesn't have your learning. You think you're too good for your own good. He's a smart feller, you know? Don't underestimate him.

PROFESSOR: You like the silly rascal, don't you?

STEWART [*laughing*]: He sees himself as my mentor.

PROFESSOR: He says you are his larney ... his white man. He owns you.

STEWART: Well, he saved me from an awkward situation at the traffic lights. After I had lost Danni and I was mindless with too much wine in my head, the Seller of Laughter came to my rescue. I think some crooks saw that I had scored big that day and got it into their heads that they were going to beat the hell out of me and grab my loot. And they did. They could have killed me if the Seller of Laughter had not come running and yelling 'Police! Police!' The bastards ran away, leaving me there for dead. That's how the Seller of Laughter brought me to this park and nursed my wounds. You can't blame him for claiming ownership of me.

PROFESSOR: And you decided to stay.

STEWART: Why not? It's as good a place as any. In this whole country – every square inch of it – I am an oppressed person, my dear Professor. First I was oppressed by the Afrikaners; now I am oppressed by your people.

PROFESSOR: Get over it, Lord Stewart. Your folks still hold

the keys to the treasure chest. You were just not smart enough to get a share of that when you had the chance. Just like I am not smart enough to get a share now that your folks find it necessary to split a tiny fraction of that treasure with the elite of my folks.

STEWART: What on earth are you on about, my dear fellow. Have you been ingesting some of my mentor's mushrooms?

PROFESSOR: I don't ingest, Lord Stewart. I eat. Only aristocrats like you ingest. And the last thing I would eat is hallucinogenic mushrooms. I may be down and out and penitent, but I'm not suicidal yet.

STEWART: Penitent. I hear that all the time. But you never say what you are penitent about.

PROFESSOR: I need to suffer in order to make good for some past I don't want to talk about. It is nobody's business but my own. It is something that is between me and my conscience. But, oh, it is eating me every waking moment of my life. There are things you don't want to talk about too because they are your own business. Danni, for instance.

STEWART: I can talk about Danni because I did nothing wrong. Tell you what, you tell me the cause of your penitence and I'll tell you about Danni.

PROFESSOR: Exchange the stories of our foolishness? Go ahead, I am all ears.

STEWART: Danielle! She was the most beautiful girl you've ever met.

PROFESSOR: Danielle? I never met her.

STEWART: That's Danni to you. And of course you never met

her. But you'd have loved her, Professor. She was a lady. She was a beautiful Afrikaner princess.

PROFESSOR: I didn't know Afrikaners have royalty.

STEWART: Actually she was a French princess. You know mos some Afrikaners have French roots. But she was more than just a princess, my Danni. She had the ancient art of hearing voices which no one else could hear. She told me that it started with her at an early age, when she was a baby, but she never thought there was anything strange about it. She thought that everyone heard voices; everyone had a party in her head. At first the voices were soft and gave her simple commands in a simple, childish language. But as she grew older the voices became elaborate. For a long time she told no one about them. Instead, she fell in love with them because they were a force for good. She kept them secret; she was afraid her folks would think she was insane and send her to a mental institution.

PROFESSOR: How did you deal with that, Lord Stewart?

STEWART: Oh, no, this was before I knew her! I met her long after that. After she had become a stock market analyst and the voices had terrorised her out of her job. Her family and colleagues asked her to deny the voices ... to suppress them. That's when they began to terrorise her. They would spin her, Professor, spin her around like a top. That I saw with my own eyes. Spinning and spinning and spinning ...

At this he twirls like a ballerina, pirouetting en pointe while at the same time calling to Danni.

Danni! Stop! What is wrong, Danielle? Stop!

He stops suddenly. He is out of breath.

I reached for her and grabbed her and held her to myself. 'Don't you worry, Danni. Everything will be fine. The damn voices will leave you one day and everything will be fine.' She turned on me angrily and said: 'I don't want them to stop. They are my voices.' Whereas I thought they were a sign of illness she saw them as a gift. Sometimes the voices came in the guise of particular saints. She was a devout Catholic so she knew all sorts of saints.

PROFESSOR: Is there such a creature as an Afrikaner Catholic?

STEWART: Of course there is such a creature as a Catholic Afrikaner. She had long converted from the stubborn faith of her French Huguenot ancestors to the Roman Catholic Church precisely because the Catholics were more tolerant of her voices. Her people, on the other hand, were busy sending her to doctors who labelled her voices 'verbal auditory hallucination' and tried to suppress them with medication. To her they were saintly voices ... voices of angels.

PROFESSOR: Doctors are the enemies of prophets.

STEWART: I met Danni at the traffic lights. She was standing there like a princess, with her bowl extended in supplication. She didn't carry any sign at all. Her bowl spoke for itself and motorists filled it with coins – even an occasional banknote. We hit it off immediately, our whiteness among all the black faces bringing us together. She liked me even more when she discovered that I treated her voices with respect. I wished I could experience their pleasantness too.

PROFESSOR: They were all in her head ... those voices.

STEWART: We are not talking of voices in the head here,

Professor. We are not talking of thoughts. These were loud voices that she could hear as if somebody had spoken.

PROFESSOR: But you never heard them yourself?

STEWART: Only she could hear them. Often she had pleasant conversations with her voices. If we had stayed together I was hoping that I would hear the voices too. Maybe my voices would merge with her voices into one big divine voice.

PROFESSOR: Yours is a beautiful story, Lord Stewart. Mine is a shameful one. It shall not be told.

STEWART: I must find Danielle.

PROFESSOR: It refuses to be told.

STEWART: I must find her, Professor.

PROFESSOR: It should never be told.

STEWART [*with greater urgency*]: I am going to find her. I am going on a pilgrimage to Benoni. I am going to receive my blessings from Francesca Zackey so that the Virgin Mary, Our Lady of Benoni, can help me find my Danielle. She was a good person, my Danni. She cannot linger in the wilderness. Our Lady of Benoni must lead me to her.

He exits.

PROFESSOR: It will never be told.

Lights fade to black.

Scene 2

The park. Lights come up on LORD STEWART. He is searching for something among the flowers. He finds it and we see that it is a mushroom. He titters and skips joyfully to the swing. As the swing sways he chews on the mushroom. His expression shows that he is not enjoying it. There are some pieces of greasy paper strewn on the grass in front of the bench. MADLOMO enters from the opposite side. She has on an orange overall and wears a plastic bag on her head as she would a headdress. She is holding an open black garbage bag with one hand and collects pieces of litter with the other, using a long wire rod with a sharp point – poker-like. LORD STEWART is looking in her direction. He giggles. Then he breaks into silly laughter.

MADLOMO: *Yho! Wangihlek'umlungu!*

LORD STEWART, looking dazed, is staring at her. His laughter has frozen on his face and now looks like a snarl.What are you looking at?

STEWART: I don't know what I was doing eating this crap. It lifts my spirits for a while and then leaves me in the dumps. I'm in the dumps, lady, so don't you pick on me.

MADLOMO: *You* were staring at me.

STEWART: Because you're a beautiful princess with colours of the rainbow all over your sexy body.

MADLOMO: Pervert!

STEWART: And the sun reflects so gloriously on your plastic headdress. It is like a halo.

17

MADLOMO: You've made this place dirty. You people, *aniz'thandi nix*. You dump litter all over the place. What do you think those dustbins are made for?

STEWART: If we keep the place clean you lose your job. I, His Royal Highness Lord Stewart, keep you employed. You should thank me.

MADLOMO [*picking up the papers*]: *Ngabelungu abanjani laba*?

STEWART: Here, try these. They will brighten your day. They'll make you see the colours of the rainbow. [*He hands her a piece of mushroom, but she ignores it.*] Suit yourself. Maybe I didn't eat enough of these things for them to give me a happy and lasting high as they do with the Seller of Laughter.

He stuffs the mushroom into his mouth, chews and then swallows quite ostentatiously.

MADLOMO: *Angizidli izinkowankowane namakhowe mina.* I am not a mad animal that eats mushrooms.

STEWART: These are not just mushrooms. They are magic mushrooms.

MADLOMO: I've come here to work for my child, not to eat mushrooms.

STEWART: You're new here, aren't you? What on earth did they do with the old nice cleaners who were always smiling and joking? *Wena ka lo* sourpuss.

MADLOMO: *Yho*! *Wang'thuka ke manje umlungu. Uthi ngiyi-poes*?

PROFESSOR enters. He is carrying a whole stack of books and newspapers. LORD STEWART tries to hide all traces of the mushroom and the fact that he was eating it.

STEWART: Ah, my dear Professor. We have a new maid cleaning our house. But she doesn't do windows.

MADLOMO: *U-maid ngunyoko.*

STEWART: The rainbow lady is talking rainbow language. What's she saying?

PROFESSOR: You don't want to know.

He arranges the books on the bench.

STEWART: How's the Johannesburg Library these days? I used to hang out there too, you know, when I was still a member of the idle rich.

After arranging his books PROFESSOR looks up and his eyes meet those of MADLOMO. Both are dumbfounded for a while, and then ...

MADLOMO: What are my eyes showing me?

PROFESSOR: MaDlomo! *Nguwe lona?*

MADLOMO: Yes, it's me. What are you doing here?

PROFESSOR [*to STEWART*]: This is MaDlomo. She is a woman from my village, KwaVimba, in KwaZulu-Natal. You don't age, even after all these years!

MADLOMO: What would I age for when you haven't aged yourself?

PROFESSOR: Oh, no, I am much younger than you. [*To STEWART*] I used to drink at her shebeen in KwaVimba. She brewed the best sorghum beer in the entire Valley of a Thousand Hills.

STEWART: You used to drink? Then where did you go wrong? Now you despise those of us who occasionally get drunk?

MADLOMO: He was a champion drunkard. And then one day he just disappeared from the village; no one knew where he went. Your people talk of you as if you had joined the World of *Amadlozi*.

PROFESSOR: They know very well that I am still alive. They shouldn't pretend they don't know why I left.

MADLOMO: I think it's ten years or more since you left. *Ngiyabona ke manje ukuthi nihlala nabelungu la eGoli*; that's why you don't want to go back home.

STEWART: What's she beefing about?

PROFESSOR: That I don't return to my home village because I am basking in the prestige of staying with white people here in Johannesburg – meaning you. [*To MADLOMO*] Lord Stewart is no longer a white man. He used to be white. But, as you can see, the sun has done its business on his skin. He's now a brown man.

STEWART [*to MADLOMO*]: Don't listen to him. The sun may have crapped on my face but I am a white man and you'd better remember that. You don't get uppity with me and start calling me names in your tribal jargon. [*To PROFESSOR*] That's what she was doing before you came ... blaming me for making the park dirty.

PROFESSOR: The colonial man in you will not die even long after the sun has set on the British Empire, Lord Stewart. Fancy, calling the language of the great amaZulu tribal jargon!

MADLOMO: I would go home if I were you. Why make yourself suffer here in eGoli when your father has a kraal full of cattle? Soon he'll be gone and the vultures who are your uncles will descend and feed on the carcass. If that happens you will not get even a single ox. You know how greedy our people are.

PROFESSOR: They will do so in any case, and that will be their business, not yours or mine.

MADLOMO: *Hawu, kade bengizingene ngani izindaba zabantu*? I don't have time to waste on idle talk. I have a park to clean; I have a demonstration to attend.

STEWART: Ah, so you are one of the municipal workers who toyi-toyi all the time, overturning dustbins and making the whole city filthy, so that you have something to clean again next time. Clever! Clever! You people know how to create work for yourselves. Yet you are busy bitching about me for one or two pieces of paper from my fish and chips.

PROFESSOR: She's right. You know we agreed that we would always keep our surroundings clean.

MADLOMO: And I am not overturning dustbins. Our demonstration is for justice.

STEWART: You must have been a schoolmaster in your previous life … keeping the surroundings clean.

PROFESSOR [*to MADLOMO*]: What's the struggle about this time? More pay and fewer hours?

MADLOMO: Our demonstration is in defence of our leader – the Right Reverend Chief Comrade my Leader, who is being accused by some *isifebe* woman of raping her.

PROFESSOR: You are the women who are demonstrating in front of the courthouse in support of the priest who is on trial for rape?

STEWART: I saw it in one of your papers.

PROFESSOR: Since when do you read newspapers, Lord Stewart?

STEWART: I stopped reading papers because I got despondent about the news of all the wholesale theft and corruption of your people in government. But once in a while I peek at the headlines when they wrap my fish and chips in the paper ... especially since you fight like a bitch when anyone touches your newspaper. So I know all about your priests and politicians who rape women.

MADLOMO: Whether you like it or not, they are yours too. And they didn't rape anybody. The Right Reverend Chief Comrade my Leader cannot rape. We are there to see to it that justice is served. We are going to sing and dance outside that courtroom until the judges find him not guilty.

PROFESSOR: What if they don't?

STEWART: After all, he admits that he did the nookie-nookie but claims it was by mutual consent.

MADLOMO: And what has that got to do with rape? Nobody is going to find him guilty of anything. We are going to see to that. You don't think we are just there to while away time, do you? Some of us are working people and have children. I have a sick daughter at home, suffering from AIDS. I am the only one who takes care of her. Despite that I must sacrifice some of the time to demonstrate at the courthouse. I start work very early cleaning the parks so that I can leave early enough to be present at the demonstration. And you know why I do that? Simply because the Right Reverend Chief Comrade my Leader is innocent.

PROFESSOR: If he's innocent, whether you're there or not the court will come to that conclusion.

MADLOMO: No, it won't. It is important that we, the women

of South Africa, put pressure on those white judges to respect our culture. And *futhi ke* the Right Reverend Chief Comrade my Leader must see that he has our full support. He must take courage every morning he walks into that courtroom to face those white judges and prosecutors. He stood with us when our culture was under siege. He came out in support of virginity testing when other leaders were hiding their heads in the sand on the matter. Now that he is under siege from the enemies of our culture we are going to stand with him.

PROFESSOR [*to STEWART*]: MaDlomo was our village's virginity tester. She was a leading virginity tester, respected in the entire Valley of a Thousand Hills.

STEWART: A woman in search of the hymen. [*With mock deference*] I bow before thee.

MADLOMO: Suka! You are a white man. You know nothing about our culture.

PROFESSOR: A woman in search of the hymen? But I thought Vesalius had found it already, in the sixteenth century.

STEWART: I knew you would have a story about it, my dear Professor. These tomes that you tote from the Johannesburg Library are not for nothing. Who was Vesalius?

MADLOMO: *Angiyihlalel'imibhedo ke mina.* I'm going. What do men know about virginity anyway?

She drags her garbage bag and starts to go. But we can see that she is curious to hear what the men are saying. She pretends to be dislodging a stubborn piece of litter with her poker tool while she listens.

PROFESSOR: He's the man MaDlomo's profession should thank for discovering the hymen in 1544. Vesalius was just the name his Latin buddies gave him; his real name was Andreas van Wesel.

STEWART: An Afrikaner! Trust an Afrikaner to discover the hymen!

PROFESSOR: He was actually Belgian, Lord Stewart. Must have been Flemish. But he was working in Pisa in Italy as an anatomist and physician at the time. He carved up a 36-year-old nun who had died of pleurisy, and discovered the hymen. To make sure that it was not just a fluke he carved up a 17-year-old hunchback girl he had stolen from the Camposanto medieval cemetery and once more located the hymen. I think MaDlomo and members of her trade should make Vesalius their patron saint.

MADLOMO cannot help but respond.

MADLOMO: When your Vesalius discovered the hymen our ancestors knew about it already.

She exits in a huff.

PROFESSOR: Of all the parks in the world, she had to work at this one! I cannot stay here any more, Lord Stewart. I must leave. I must find a new refuge.

STEWART: Leave? Just because of her? What has she got on you?

PROFESSOR: I don't like people from home hovering around where I am. There is a reason why I left them back there. Now she's going to gossip about me and everyone back at KwaVimba will know my business.

STEWART: So you're going to pack and go, just like that?

PROFESSOR: You don't know these people, Lord Stewart.

STEWART: You make me suspicious, Professor. You're running away from something.

PROFESSOR: I am not running away from anything, man. Why would I run away?

STEWART: You just said you are leaving.

PROFESSOR: Leaving is not running away. It's just that I cannot tolerate her here.

STEWART: Like she has something on you?

PROFESSOR: When did you become so smart-alecky?

STEWART: She said something about your people back in the village? What did she mean, exactly?

PROFESSOR: Hey, why didn't you ask her? She said it, I didn't.

STEWART: Who are you, Professor?

PROFESSOR: Oh, to hell with you, man! Have I asked who you are?

STEWART: You know who I am. I told you about Danielle and her voices. You didn't tell me a damn thing except to say that your story must never be told.

PROFESSOR: So you reckon that when you were telling me about Danielle you were telling me about yourself?

STEWART: Who exactly are you, Professor?

PROFESSOR does not respond.

> And how come you always have money? Your father is rich, hey, with lots of cattle? That's what the woman said. Is that where you get your money? The old man sends you money from home, does he?

PROFESSOR: I don't get a single cent from home. As far as they are concerned I might as well be dead.

STEWART: So what's your source of riches? Come on, Professor, tell us. Don't be selfish.

PROFESSOR: You can hardly call it riches.

STEWART: How come you always have money, and yet no one has ever seen you work at the traffic lights like we do.

PROFESSOR [*irritated*]: I get it from the government, if you must know.

STEWART: You work for the government? How? When? Doing what?

PROFESSOR: I don't work for the government. I get a disability grant.

STEWART: But you're not disabled! Or are you? Where?

PROFESSOR: Since when did you become my interrogator?

STEWART: I want a government grant too. I want to be like you. I was born to be the idle rich like you. Why else do you think I ennobled myself? Because I knew that I was destined to be in the ranks of the idle rich. You got to help me, Professor.

PROFESSOR: It was not easy, Lord Stewart. I had to buy sputum from a sick man.

STEWART: You got rich from trading in sputum?

PROFESSOR: Exactly. Back in the village a relative of mine became known throughout the Valley of a Thousand Hills as a seller of saliva. He was sick with TB, which the doctors found difficult to heal because he had AIDS. He was on antiretrovirals and was getting a disability grant from the government. But he was a resourceful man and the grant was not enough to support his many wives and mistresses. So he earned more money by selling his saliva. He had a sign on the door with prices for the day: 'Buy Saliva Cheap – Special Sale Price R30.00'. He sat on a stool in the middle of his hut and waited for the customers. They came and paid and he drew the biggest chunks of phlegm from the depth of his soul. You go to the clinic and tell them of your persistent and unceasing cough. They give you a small glass container and ask you to fill it with sputum. You already have the sputum in your pocket from the seller of saliva; all you do is to transfer it to their container. And behold! The tests show you have the worst kind of TB imaginable. So, Lord Stewart, that is exactly what I did.

STEWART: What if they admit you to the hospital? What about the treatment?

PROFESSOR: Hospitals are full, Lord Stewart. They no longer have the luxury of admitting you for TB. They gave me treatment but I dumped it into a pit latrine. After six months I got more saliva and the doctors said my TB is resistant to treatment.

STEWART: When another six months is over you'll have to go back to your village again for more saliva?

PROFESSOR: Oh, no, the guy who initially sold me sputum died. There are many other people who sell sputum all over these days ... even in the townships here. Saliva is big business if you know where to go.

STEWART: No wonder your conscience is eating you. So, that's the story that must never be told. That's what your penitence is all about.

PROFESSOR [*laughing mockingly*]: Far from it, Lord Stewart.
I have no regrets about the disability grant. It is my
share of the national cake. Why should it only be
politicians and civil servants who loot the national
coffers? I must also have my share. The disability grant
is the last thing to give me sleepless nights. The only
thing, Lord Stewart, that gives me sleepless nights
is how to sustain my disability forever so that the
fountain does not run dry.

The SELLER OF LAUGHTER bursts in, effervescent as ever.

SELLER: You guys, you'll get old before your time sitting here
like pumpkins. There's life out there. And what's with
you, Lord Stewart? I didn't see you at the traffic lights
today? *U lelofa jwale monna kea u bona*!

STEWART: I had planned to go to Benoni.

SELLER: Are there more profitable traffic lights in Benoni?

STEWART: No, man. To see Francesca Zackey for the blessings
of the Virgin.

PROFESSOR: What happened?

STEWART: I didn't go. I didn't have enough money for the
taxi. When I came back here I thought I'd borrow some
money from you, my dear Professor, but you had gone
to the library. Then there was that impertinent woman
from your village.

*The SELLER OF LAUGHTER walks to the flowers and searches
among them.*

PROFESSOR: Our Lady of Benoni; you think she'll make
Danni come back to you?

STEWART: With Danni gone I have learnt that sometimes

we take a person for granted because we think she will always be with us. Then all of a sudden she is not there. Maybe she's gone to a place where she thinks she won't be taken for granted any more. We flounder, we are lost, we sail hesitantly through life …

SELLER: Now you tell me, you bastards, who stole my zoomer?

He glares at PROFESSOR.

PROFESSOR: Don't look at me. What would I need mushrooms for?

SELLER: I had one that was ready to eat. This morning I said goodbye to it, knowing that I would come back to use it this evening. And it is not there. It can only be one of you, you old bastards. Or both of you.

STEWART: No, no, it can't be Professor. He doesn't steal from his friends. None of us does. Maybe it's some wild animal … maybe some rabbit came and ate it. I hear rabbits are partial to mushrooms.

SELLER [*despondent*]: What will I do without my zoomers? I need them for inspiration. How do I create the Mother of All Jokes without my inspiration?

STEWART: By tomorrow morning they'll have grown again.

SELLER: I don't need one tomorrow. I need one now.

PROFESSOR: Your friends – *intanga zakho* – out there sniff glue for inspiration.

SELLER: I am not some cheap street kid *wena. Ha ke malala-phayiphu.*

He goes to the merry-go-round, pushes it with great anger, then jumps on it for a ride. He is letting off steam. But the equipment won't cooperate. It squeaks to an abrupt stop. Something has broken.

STEWART: That's the new South Africa for you. That's what happens to everything you people touch; it breaks.

PROFESSOR: For how long will your bitterness about your people losing the monopoly of power last, Lord Stewart?

SELLER: Don't gloat. It has done this before. I know how to fix it. Tomorrow it will be running smoothly again. And tomorrow I'll have a new crop of zoomers. Don't you dare steal them again, you old bastards.

PROFESSOR: You know why the Mother of All Jokes will never be there? Because you have no respect for your elders. Inspiration never comes to little twerps who are disrespectful.

SELLER: I know you wish that I'll fail in my mission to create the best joke of all. But I won't. I am determined to succeed. With the help of people like Lord Stewart I will succeed.

STEWART: How do I help? [*Humouring him*] I'll do anything for you, my mentor.

SELLER: Maybe we should be a team when we go out there to beg. You be my slave in chains; I'll be the slave master. I'll have a board which reads: 'Slave Master Fallen on Hard Times. Needs Money to Feed Slave'. There! Don't you think that's brilliant. We'll make a lot of money.

STEWART: No one will believe you. I'm white, you're black. The world over, whiteness is power; blackness is servitude.

PROFESSOR: Maybe that's why it's a good joke. There, you

see? You thought of something clever without your mushrooms.

SELLER: Nobody asked you. This is between me and Lord Stewart. You wouldn't know a damn thing about it; you've never worked the traffic lights.

He exits.

PROFESSOR: Hey, I was supporting you!

STEWART: You'll never win with that one, Professor. He'll only appreciate you when you're gone. He does not know that soon he'll be wishing he had not taken you for granted.

PROFESSOR: Soon? But I'm not going anywhere?

STEWART: You are going away; you said so. You're running away from the virginity tester.

PROFESSOR: Okay, I am staying put. After all I came here first. If there's anyone who must leave it's her. She'll have to find a job elsewhere. I must find a way to scare her away.

STEWART: So, a bull and a cow from the Valley of a Thousand Hills cannot be in the same kraal. [*Jokingly*] Do you think she'll get ideas about testing your virginity, Professor? I never hear you talk of women. Maybe you've not been deflowered yet? Otherwise why don't you want to share a park with a virginity tester?

PROFESSOR: I am no fan of her profession, that's all.

STEWART: I think it's a noble profession.

PROFESSOR: What is it with men and virginity anyway? What is this fascination? Virgins have determined the history of the world. People even wage war on their

31

behalf. Men kill other human beings so that when they get to Paradise they can have a roll in the hay with 72 virgins. Not just 72 women. Seventy-two *virgins*.

STEWART: What do you do with 72 virgins in Heaven? Don't tell me folks do the nookie-nookie in Heaven. And with so much libido too that they need 72!

PROFESSOR: It must be recreational. I don't think procreation happens over there.

STEWART: But 72! That's greedy, my dear Professor!

PROFESSOR: Don't be too smug about it, Lord Stewart. Your faith has its fair share of virgins as well. I am giving you money to go see one in Benoni tomorrow.

STEWART [*making the sign of the cross*]: Forgive me, Virgin Mary Mother of Jesus. This talk is becoming too blasphemous for my liking.

PROFESSOR: Suit yourself. You brought the virgins up, I didn't.

STEWART: I am not saying you shouldn't give me money to go to Benoni. I just don't want to talk about virgins any more.

There is a pregnant silence. And then ...

Do you know that Danni was a virgin?

PROFESSOR: What? She was with you all that time and she was a virgin?

STEWART: Three years we begged together. I never touched her. And no one had touched her before me. She was untouched. Danni was one of thousands of Catholic women worldwide who have consecrated their virginity to God.

PROFESSOR: *Hawu, kanti* Danielle was a nun?

STEWART: Oh, no, she was not a nun. These are ordinary women who belong to the Rite for the Consecration of Virgins Living in the World. That's their organisation. Danni told me it was only founded by the church in 1970 and her voices commanded her to join it. These women are not nuns at all, Professor. They take no vows or join any monastic order. They are ordinary women living ordinary lives, except for the fact that they have promised their virginity to God. That is why Danni never married.

PROFESSOR: Now I see why you believe the pilgrimage to Benoni will help you get her back. The Virgin of Benoni will help you find your lost virgin.

STEWART: Virgins are magical beings, Professor, and my Danni was a magical woman. Come here; I want to show you something.

He leads him to the flowers. From among the Easter flowers he takes out a plastic bag.

PROFESSOR: I see that you and the Seller of Laughter stash your loot among the flowers.

STEWART: No one bothers with flowers. You know what this is?

He shows him something he has taken from the plastic bag. Obviously to LORD STEWART this is a solemn moment and PROFESSOR accords it its due respect.

PROFESSOR: It's a slice of toast and a potato crisp.

STEWART: Not just any toast. Not just any potato crisp. Danni was prone to identifying the Virgin Mary and her Son in everyday things. Look at this Simba chip carefully.

What do you see? Don't you see the image? It is
shaped like the face of Jesus Christ. Danni discovered
it in a packet we were eating three years ago. She
immediately identified the face of Jesus Christ on it.
We have been keeping it ever since. When it turned
red in places she said it was the stigmata.

PROFESSOR: And the toasted bread?

STEWART: Sometimes she helped with the cooking at the
Salvation Army Homeless Shelter. One day she was
preparing breakfast. When the toast popped out it had
an image of the Virgin Mary impressed on it. See?
Well, you may not see it very clearly now, but it used to
be much sharper. It has faded with time.

PROFESSOR: And you've kept these all this time in memory
of Danni?

STEWART: I have kept these all these years in memory of
Danni.

PROFESSOR: You must go to Benoni tomorrow. Francesca
must help you to see the Virgin live. I am sure she'll be
pleased to meet you, especially after you have kept her
pictures on bread and potato crisps.

STEWART: Only on the toast. On the potato chip it is her son ...
with stigmata.

PROFESSOR: Still, the Virgin will be excited to see you.

STEWART: You are the man, Professor! You are the man!

Lights fade to black.

Scene 3

Lights rise on PROFESSOR. He is sitting on a bench reading a newspaper. The SELLER OF LAUGHTER is hammering away at the merry-go-round, trying to fix it. He is making quite a racket with his hammer, occasionally stealing a look at PROFESSOR to see whether he is irritated out of his wits. Seeing that PROFESSOR is ignoring the racket, he hammers even louder. When it gets too loud PROFESSOR stands up and takes a few steps towards a flat cardboard sign lying face down on the grass. He turns it face up and reads it. The SELLER OF LAUGHTER stops hammering and rushes to get his board.

SELLER: Hey, what do you think you're doing?

PROFESSOR [*reading aloud*]: 'Are you going to spare me some coins or do you want me to reach for my dark glasses and white cane?'

SELLER: Give me my sign back, you old bastard!

PROFESSOR: Is this the Mother of All Jokes? The joke that's going to make you millions?

SELLER snatches the sign away from PROFESSOR.

SELLER: You have no right to read my private things!

PROFESSOR: The joke that you will franchise to other beggars in other parts of the city? That's going to grace traffic lights in some of the most upmarket suburbs of Johannesburg?

SELLER: There is nothing wrong with this joke. You're just
jealous, that's all.

PROFESSOR: The joke that's going to kill the *ngamlas* with
laughter even at the traffic lights of neighbouring
towns – from Benoni to Boksburg?

SELLER [*defiantly*]: Yeah, it is the joke. So what?

PROFESSOR: There is nothing original about it. It's a take on
the old standard: 'Are you going to give me money or
do you want me to fake a limp?' I thought you were
planning to come with something groundbreaking!

SELLER: Who cares for originality? I want a joke that's going
to make me money, that's all. Back in the Free State
we say *thebe e sehelwa hodim'a engwe*. We build new
things from what others before us have created.

PROFESSOR: If you want to make people laugh you need
something new. Every Jo'burg motorist has seen this
one.

SELLER: In a different form. Limping is not the same as being
blind.

Enter LORD STEWART. He goes straight to his swing.

PROFESSOR: But the same idea. If you want to be a
millionaire you will have to think of something better.
Like the joke you had in mind involving Lord Stewart
and the advantages provided by his whiteness.

STEWART: Hey, don't involve me in that. I'm not going to be
dragged in chains in the streets of Johannesburg. I
don't want to be the joke. I still have my self-respect,
you know?

SELLER: Please, please, please, Lord Stewart. It's going to be a great performance that's going to surpass all their signs put together.

PROFESSOR: How did things go in Benoni; you're back early. I didn't know Francesca and her Virgin Mary doled out fast-food blessings.

SELLER holds the swing still.

SELLER: Come on, Lord Stewart! There's money to be made here!

STEWART [*angry*]: Just let it rest, man! Can't you see when a man wants to be left alone? I went all the way to Benoni for nothing and I don't have the patience for any of your ... Okay, sorry, man, but let's just let it rest. Okay?

SELLER's feelings are hurt. He goes to the merry-go-round and tinkers with it, but not as loudly this time.

Can you imagine this? The Virgin Mary has strict business hours and I missed them by a day. There is a sign at the Zackey family home: 'Greetings family and friends. Thanks for visiting the home of "Our Lady of the Ray". Please note the following times for prayer and spiritual healing: Monday and Wednesday 3pm until 5pm and 7pm until 9pm. Saturday 2pm to 6pm. Thank you and God bless you. Francesca.'

PROFESSOR: She keeps real tight hours, doesn't she?

STEWART: Now I'll never find Danni.

The SELLER OF LAUGHTER tests his handiwork. The merry-go-round is working. He pushes it and then rides. At the same time LORD STEWART is swaying gently on the swing. For a while there is no joy in the eyes of the two men on the playground equipment; they act as though they are forced to be where they are. PROFESSOR breaks the silence.

PROFESSOR: Tomorrow is Wednesday; the Virgin will be on
        duty. I'll give you more money and you'll go to Benoni.

STEWART [*excited*]: Long live the sputum!

He jumps down from the swing and embraces PROFESSOR. The
SELLER OF LAUGHTER is not impressed. He leaves his merry-
go-round turning on its own until it stops, while he takes his
sign from the grass.

SELLER: You're all full of it. *Le masepa kaofela.*

He exits.

PROFESSOR: When your Danielle returns try to keep her
        happy this time, hey? Don't do whatever it was that
        made her leave.

STEWART: I didn't do anything wrong, Professor. I was just
        being a man. A man has needs, Professor, especially
        when he has to spend day after day and night after
        night with a fine woman like Danni. I hoped one day
        she would break her resolve and we would make love
        like all normal couples do. I kept on bothering her …
        cajoling … pleading … begging … then threatening.

PROFESSOR: Threatening? With force?

STEWART: No, no, Professor. I am a gentleman. Threatening
        to find sex from the prostitutes of Hillbrow. I hoped to
        break her resistance.

PROFESSOR: You couldn't come to terms with her virginity,
        then?

STEWART: At first I understood it because it was a command
        from her voices. But when God put man and woman on
        this world, Professor, and gave them different organs
        he was not making a mistake. He wanted them to

38

use those organs. I am a man, Professor, so I kept on pestering Danni just for a little nookie-nookie. Maybe I finally got on her nerves.

PROFESSOR: So, one day she packed and left?

STEWART: It was not as ceremonious as that. She had nothing to pack. I lost Danni at the traffic lights. One cold afternoon a car with three men stopped. I can still see it even as I stand here. It was a red Toyota Camry. They beckoned Danni and she smiled. I thought they wanted to give her some money. She walked to the car, but instead of giving her money they opened the door and enticed her into the back. She hesitated a bit and then pulled her coat around her, preparing to get in.

He role-plays himself and Danielle at the traffic lights.

'No, Danni, don't go! Don't get into that car!'

'My voices, they tell me to go!'

'You don't know who those men are, Danni! You don't know what they're going to do to you!'

By this time she was already getting into the car. I had reached the car too and was pushing my way inside.

'My voices are never wrong, Lord Stewart.'

The traffic light turned green and the cars behind were hooting like mad. You know how impatient Johannesburg drivers are. [*He imitates hooters and giving the finger.*] Up yours too, mate! They didn't care about Danni and that the men were kidnapping her. All they cared about was that the robot was green and their time was being wasted. The men

pushed me out of the car and sped away. I
rolled on the tarmac. It was just luck that the
other cars didn't run me over.

PROFESSOR: And that was the last time you saw Danni?

STEWART: That was the last time. I went to the police and told
them Danni had been kidnapped. 'Who are you?' they
asked. 'What relationship did you have with her?' I told
them. And I told them how special Danni was. They
were dismissive of the whole thing. Danni was just a
woman I had met at the traffic lights, they said. She got
into the car of her own accord, they said. 'You tell us
you don't know who those men are or how she's related
to them. She is an adult. She can go with any man she
wants.' And for them that was the end of the story. But
for me, my dear Professor, it was not the end. I was
hurting, and I am still hurting to this day.

*PROFESSOR gives him a comforting hug. MADLOMO enters,
cleaning up the litter as usual with her poker.*

MADLOMO: *Cha ke manje ningohlule! Yiyo kanti into oyihlalele
la eGoli? Ukugonana nabelungu?*

STEWART: You're late for work today.

MADLOMO: Yho! Are you my boss now?

STEWART: Yes, I am your boss. As a taxpayer I am your boss.

PROFESSOR [*laughs*]: Taxpayer, Lord Stewart? When last did
you pay your taxes?

STEWART: When I was working I paid them like clockwork.
Before your affirmative action kicked me out of my job
at the South African Railways and Harbours. I'm still a
taxpayer at heart, and therefore I'm her boss.

40

PROFESSOR: If you worked for the South Africa Railways and Harbours, you lost your job before we took over so you can't blame affirmative action. I, on the other hand, can, because it affirms friends and family and cronies of the high and mighty while the rest of us black folks remain poor and unemployed.

MADLOMO: I knew you'd end up blaming the government for your laziness.

PROFESSOR: *Phela wena*, you have a job, MaDlomo.

STEWART: And you are late.

MADLOMO: *Yini ngawe kanti*? I do my work even when I'm late. I am late for a good reason. I went to the demonstration at the courthouse.

PROFESSOR: Ah, the rape case of the Right Reverend Chief Comrade my Leader is still going on and you put it above your job!

MADLOMO: I am doing it for South Africa.

STEWART: This man has raped a woman and you're doing it for South Africa?

PROFESSOR: Alleged! Careful now. He has not been found guilty.

MADLOMO: And he won't be found guilty as long as we are there every day to remind those white judges and prosecutors that we own this country now. And to remind the woman *oqambh'amanga ngaye* that the women of South Africa condemn her and stand behind our pastor and leader.

PROFESSOR: I can understand your support of your leader.

But I don't understand why you insult the accuser –
blaming the victim.

MADLOMO: What kind of a woman accuses her elders of
rape? There is something greater at stake here than
her personal pride as an individual woman who is
alleged to have been violated.

STEWART: I don't see anything greater. I wouldn't have forced
myself on Danielle.

MADLOMO [*ignoring STEWART*]: After all, we all know that
men are dogs and nothing will ever change that. Who
of us has not had men force themselves on her?

STEWART: Danni! Danni! I never forced myself on Danni.
Maybe I should have done like the Right Reverend
Chief Comrade my Leader.

*LORD STEWART is obviously distressed at the thought of
Danielle and what he has lost by not forcing himself on her. He
goes to his comforting swing and sways gently to calm himself
down.*

PROFESSOR: In other words, MaDlomo, you've all been raped
at one time or another and ...

MADLOMO: Only a woman who is a sissy will complain
about it. Real women don't cry rape. They stand up,
brush the dust from their kangas and move on. The
Right Reverend Chief Comrade my Leader stands for
something greater than just having sex with a woman.
He stands for the people ... the poor ... those who have
been let down by a government that has failed to
deliver.

PROFESSOR: *Chaaa*! *Weeee*! *MaDlomo, nguwe lo osho nje*?

MADLOMO: She should feel honoured to be raped by a great

man like the Right Reverend Comrade my Leader.
What has the world come to? How times have changed!
In our days this whole silly mess would not have been
an issue at all, and the woman would actually be
boasting about it instead of complaining to the white
man's court.

PROFESSOR [*as if asking the audience*]: Where is the women's
league of the liberation movement when women are
uttering such statements?

MADLOMO: Uttering such statements? What do you mean
'uttering such statements'? Don't you understand what
I am trying to drum into your thick skull?

PROFESSOR: I'll tell you where they are: busy protecting
their Cabinet jobs, or angling for deployments into
the lucrative civil service and parastatals, busy
accumulating wealth through some BEE scheme. For
them there'll always be something greater at stake
than standing up for the rights of women. It was like
that even during the days of the liberation struggle.
They turned a blind eye to rape and other forms of
sexual abuse at refugee and guerrilla camps and in
exile because there was something greater at stake:
national liberation. So, their own struggle for gender
equality had to take a back seat. It will always take
a back seat, because there will always be something
greater at stake!

MADLOMO: Since when have you become a spokesman for
women? Do you think we have no voices to speak
for ourselves? You should be fighting for the Right
Reverend Chief Comrade my Leader too because he
is fighting for your rights. When he takes over this
country you'll have a job instead of sitting in the park
eating your own lice. In any case that woman was not
even a virgin. She had done it before.

PROFESSOR: Aha! It had to come back to virginity. I don't
understand your obsession with virginity, MaDlomo.

STEWART: My Danni was a virgin.

MADLOMO: You, too, should be concerned with virginity.
After all, you lost a wife because of lack of it.

*This piques LORD STEWART's interest. He jumps down from his
swing and goes to the PROFESSOR.*

STEWART: Ah, Monsieur le Professeur! You had a wife and
never said a word about it?

MADLOMO [*laughs*]: So, you haven't told your friends how you
brought *ihlazo* to the family, and then ran away? [*To
STEWART*] He hasn't told you of the shame that made
him leave the village?

PROFESSOR: You don't know half the story. That's not why I
left the village.

MADLOMO: *Ucabang'ukuthi angizazi izindaba zakho wena*? I
know all about it. That is why you have all this anger
and bitterness in your heart. And now you want to take
it out on us who are working to preserve our culture.

STEWART: That's why you don't want her at this park,
Professor; she knows your secrets.

MADLOMO [*to STEWART*]: So, he does not want me here? You
can tell him that his secret is not a secret back in the
village of KwaVimba, and even in the rest of the Valley
of a Thousand Hills. People spoke about it for years.

PROFESSOR: It was the fault of people like you, who are
obsessed with virginity. No one cared about things
like that until you revived old traditions of virginity
testing that had died two centuries ago. We were living

happily in the twentieth century until you took us back to what you call our roots.

MADLOMO: Is it my fault that you married *iseqamgwaqo* – a tainted woman – shaming not only your parents but your village?

She leaves them and resumes picking up the litter a short distance away. But we can see that she wants to hear everything they are saying.

PROFESSOR [*calling after her*]: Thabisile was not a prostitute. That is what you people called her, but she was nothing like that.

STEWART [*amused that at last PROFESSOR'S armour is being breached*]: Where did you get that one, Professor? From Hillbrow?

PROFESSOR: She is just repeating vicious village gossip, Lord Stewart. Thabisile was a good woman from KwaVimba. We fell in love when we were both at primary school. It continued until we completed high school. She was the only one, the love of my life, the woman I was going to marry. When my uncles went to ask for her hand in marriage it was the best day of my life. Lobola was paid and our parents spared no expense in organising a big feast to celebrate our marriage in the traditional manner of amaZulu. That night was our first night.

STEWART: You mean all the years you'd been together no nookie-nookie? What kind of a boy were you?

PROFESSOR: You didn't have it with Danni. What kind of a man were you?

STEWART [*sadly*]: Danni had consecrated her virginity to God.

PROFESSOR: Thabisile had not consecrated her virginity
to anyone. She was a strict traditional Zulu girl who
wanted to wait until she was married. We petted,
though, and we did *ukusoma*. So it was not too difficult
to wait until we were married.

STEWART: *Ukusoma*?

PROFESSOR: Intercrural sex. Sex without any penetration.

STEWART: I wish Danni had allowed me to do the *ukusoma*
thing. Just once. I would not have pestered her after
that. She would still be with me.

PROFESSOR: So that night was the night. And it went
beautifully. We sent each other to the stars and
returned to earth, breathless.

STEWART: Oh, my dear Professor.

PROFESSOR: My grandmother woke us up early in the morning
and told us to vacate our room. Outside we saw a group
of other grandmothers – my relatives and neighbours.
They had come to inspect our bedding. They were
looking for the stain of blood. It was not there. They
declared that my new bride was not a virgin.

STEWART: Of course she was not. She couldn't be after you
had done the dirty deed with her the previous night.

PROFESSOR: You don't understand, Lord Stewart. They said I
married a girl who was not a virgin in the first place.
She was shamed. She was called names. Because our
sheets were stainless she was called *iseqamgwaqo*, the
very name MaDlomo called her now.

MADLOMO: Don't talk about me. I'm no longer part of that
argument. I'm doing the work of the municipality.
Ngisebenzel'izingane zami mina la kwa-maspala.

PROFESSOR: She was teased when she went to the well to draw water, she was harassed when she went to the general dealer store to buy sugar and paraffin. Her life became a nightmare. The elders demanded that she should name the man who had deflowered her so that if it was not me he should be fined a cow. She refused to name any name because she was adamant that she had never been penetrated by any man. I knew she was telling the truth. She was ostracised by the other women of the village. And my parents were ostracised too. Until they went to Thabisile's home to demand at least part of the lobola back. You know, like they had been sold damaged goods.

STEWART: And so your wife left?

PROFESSOR: What woman would stay after such shame? She left, Lord Stewart, because I did nothing. I did not speak out when an injustice was done to her. I was silent in deference to my culture and out of respect for my elders. I have regretted that silence ever since, because I lost the woman I loved. I vowed I would never be silent again.

STEWART: Whoa! My dear Professor. This virginity thing is quite heavy I must say!

PROFESSOR: Yes, I lost Thabisile because of virginity. That is why I went out in search of virginity. I wanted to understand what it is and why people are dying because of it. You see all those books? They are part of my search for virginity.

STEWART [*giggling lasciviously*]: You are searching for it in the wrong place, my dear Professor. You will not find it between the pages of books, but between the legs of girls.

47

MADLOMO cannot help but return to the men to try to put them straight.

MADLOMO: *Cha ke manje,* you are exaggerating. People dying? Nobody killed Thabisile.

PROFESSOR: They may not have killed her physically, but elsewhere people do die. In the United States, in November 2004, Jasmine Archie was murdered by her mother, who forced her to drink bleach because her mother believed she had lost her virginity. Jasmine, of Birmingham, Alabama, was only 12 years old at the time. In many countries where honour killing is part of the culture women are murdered every day by their parents for failing some virginity test.

MADLOMO [*sadly*]: I am sorry to hear of the death of the little girl. I do not think the mother was in her right senses when she did it. But you must understand, you son of KwaVimba, God gave Thabisile the gift of virginity so that she could give it to you, her husband.

PROFESSOR: Exactly. Virginity exists for the man, not the woman who's supposed to possess it. And what does the man do with it? How does he put it to use? How does it benefit him?

MADLOMO: Yhoooo! *Imihlolo!*

PROFESSOR: *Yiqiniso ke lelo,* MaDlomo. Virginity is a commodity owned by the man, the father of the daughter. It's a prize whose possession is passed from the girl's father to the husband on payment of a price.

MADLOMO: *Cha ngiyabona ke manje, ukuhlala nabelungu* has messed up your head. You even call our sacred custom of *ilobola* a price, as if a woman is being sold like a cow. That's why you spend your life in the park.

The ancestors are punishing you. [*She looks at LORD STEWART accusingly.*] *Wenziwa yilabelungu ohlala nabo.*

STEWART: Immediately she says *mlungu mlungu* I know she's blaming me for something.

MADLOMO: You are the one who messed up this man's head. He was not like this back at KwaVimba. He respected our traditions.

STEWART: He told you already; it's the books that messed his head, not me.

MADLOMO: Well, they have made him lose *ubuntu*, those books of his. Our culture *wubuntu bethu.*

PROFESSOR: If *ubuntu* means an acceptance of everything that comes under the cloak of African culture, then *ubuntu* is an instrument of oppression.

MADLOMO: It's not only the African culture that values virginity. The Bible has a lot to say about it. Even the Mother of Jesus was subjected to virginity testing by the midwife, Salome.

STEWART: The very Virgin Mary that I am going to see in Benoni? Which Bible have you been reading?

PROFESSOR: It's there all right, Lord Stewart. But it is in the Apocrypha, which are accepted by the Catholics as part of the scriptures but not by the Protestants. Salome did not believe that Mary was a virgin so she subjected her to a virginity test. But her hands were burnt by Mary's sacred genitalia until they were shrivelled like biltong.

MADLOMO: The point is, virginity testing did not start with me. It was not introduced by me into the world.

Deuteronomy made it clear that virgins like Rebecca and Maria were given important sacred duties because they were virgins, and therefore they were clean. Girls must be proud of their virginity.

PROFESSOR: What is this virginity, anyway? No one is able to tell me what it is. No one has touched it, smelled it, tasted it, heard it. It's not there. It's not anywhere. All they are able to say is what terminates it. If it was there at all before it was terminated then what was it? Where was it located exactly?

MADLOMO: You told us the other day about a white man who discovered the hymen. That's where virginity is located.

PROFESSOR: Nonsense! Girls are active. Some don't have a hymen because it has been perforated during some activity. Some were born without a hymen. If you are right when you say virginity is located at the hymen, then they are not virgins. Still that does not tell me what virginity is. It merely tells me what it is not. The hymen is the least reliable measure.

STEWART: Where is this damned hymen that's causing all these problems the world over?

PROFESSOR: It is at the very entrance of the secret garden, Lord Stewart.

MADLOMO: How would you know about it when you don't have it?

PROFESSOR: I made it my business to find out after I lost my wife to stupidity. I wanted to know why there was no stain. I knew that she was innocent, if not being a virgin is a crime at all. I learnt that some hymens can survive intercourse without breaking; they merely bend. Some are too sturdy to bleed. You cannot conclude virginity from the hymen, let alone from a bloodstain.

MADLOMO: Blood is the sign that her girlhood has been ruptured. Even the Book of Books, the Holy Bible itself, says so. In Deuteronomy Chapter 22 verse 21 it says that a girl who does not bleed on her wedding night should be stoned to death. Thabisile was lucky that the law of man, which you call the Constitution, forbids us from following the law of God as represented by the Bible.

STEWART: You are doing God's work, MaDlomo. Keep it up! Stone them to death.

MADLOMO: We amaZulu never stone anyone to death even though the Bible commands us to. *Sinobuntu.*

PROFESSOR: Thabisile proved that not every woman bleeds when having sex for the first time. In any case, not even physicians and surgeons can tell with absolute certainty whether a woman is a virgin or not. Unless they are charlatans they cannot conclude that the fact that the hymen is not intact means that the woman has had sex before. The vagina has no way of recording its sexual history.

MADLOMO: *Izinto ozikhulumayo zingavala umuntu izindlebe.*

PROFESSOR: What I'm saying, MaDlomo, is that proving virginity has never been an exact science, unless you catch someone in the sex act and actually witness penetration. Have you ever seen virginity, MaDlomo? Have you ever measured it?

MADLOMO: I don't talk about such things with men.

PROFESSOR: Just as I thought. It cannot be seen. What you look for are its signs. And how do you interpret those signs?

MADLOMO: The way my ancestors did.

PROFESSOR: Which ancestors? The ancestors are dead, MaDlomo; we are alive today in today's world. Virginity tests have not been done by our people since the days of uShaka kaSenzangakhona, 200 years ago! In his wisdom Shaka abolished the practice, in the same way that he abolished the Reed Dance and circumcision for boys. And the amaZulu people were no worse for it. Until the present-day leaders, who see it as a source of power to re-invent culture. Virginity testing can't be part of the Zulu culture if it has not been practised for 200 years. And by the way, when it was practised before the days of Shaka it was not a public spectacle like it is today. It was something private within families. Not what MaDlomo was doing at KwaVimba, a public spectacle out there in the field or in community halls.

MADLOMO: Our King has brought it back so it is now part of our culture.

PROFESSOR: I can understand why the King is re-introducing these practices. I am a Zulu child and therefore I respect *Isilo samaBandla. Bayethe, wena weZulu.*

MADLOMO: Not when you talk dirt about the culture of his people, *futhi* in front of white people.

STEWART: Hey, leave me out of your Zulu civil war. I have my own problems.

He sits on his swing and sways.

PROFESSOR: With all due respect to the King, in our modern
democracy he has no power at all; all power is with
elected political leaders. He is just a figurehead. He
must therefore create for himself new sources of
power. If he can't exercise political power then he
must exercise cultural power. He must re-invent
some pomp and ceremony over which he can preside.
The Reed Dance. Virginity testing. Circumcision for
boys. Polygamous marriages. Now we have a whole
set of new rituals over which he can be consulted
and exercise some form of authority. As a powerless
figurehead history would otherwise forget him; now it
is bound to remember him as the man who reversed
the decisions of Shaka the Great after 200 years!

*The SELLER OF LAUGHTER bursts in. He is all excitement as
usual, though we never find out what he is excited about.*

SELLER: I am on the verge of a breakthrough. Eat your hearts
out you old bastards who have been trying to work
against me.

PROFESSOR [*ignoring SELLER*]: So, *uyabona ke* MaDlomo,
lento yenu ye-virginity, virginity, culture, culture,
ayingeni ndawo la.

MADLOMO: Shhhh ... You cannot talk about such things in
the presence of a child.

She is paying closer attention to SELLER.

PROFESSOR: This one? He knows bigger things than that.
He's been around the block a few times.

MADLOMO: Whose child are you, my child?

SELLER: Hau, *mme*, you can't know my parents. They're not
from here. *Ke moshan'a Foreyisetata kwana.*

MADLOMO: You're staying with these rascals? They're going to corrupt you.

SELLER: You're right, *mme*, they're very corrupt. Especially that one they call Professor.

MADLOMO [*to PROFESSOR*]: *Uze waziwa nayizingane.* You should be ashamed of yourself. [*To SELLER*] Don't you have a home, my child?

SELLER: I grew up in the streets, *mme*. That's my home.

MADLOMO [*concerned*]: This is not a good place for a child.

STEWART: Take him with you. He does need some mothering.

SELLER: Are you selling me now, Lord Stewart? Trying to get rid of me so that I don't bother you about taking part in our joke. It will benefit you too, you know?

The SELLER OF LAUGHTER goes to his flowers, and from among them he harvests one good mushroom.

MADLOMO: And you are such a beautiful boy to waste your life with these no-good beggars. You should be at school learning something useful.

SELLER searches some more and discovers the plastic bag that we saw earlier. It contains LORD STEWART'S sacred relics. SELLER looks into the bag then puts it under his shirt. PROFESSOR has spotted him.

PROFESSOR: Hey, is that not your bread and Simba crisp he is stealing?

Too late. The SELLER OF LAUGHTER has dashed out. LORD STEWART rummages frantically through the flowers, but his plastic bag is gone.

STEWART: Bloody hell! He has stolen my things.

MADLOMO: Bread and Simba chips? Is that what you are crying for? A grown man like you *ikhalela isinkwa namaSimba*?

STEWART: You don't understand. It's not just bread and chips. That toast has the image of the Virgin Mary and the crisp has Jesus with the stigmata.

MADLOMO: *Ubheda ngani manje umlungu? uMaria uhlangana kuphi nesinkwa*?

STEWART: I am going to kill that boy with my bare hands!

MADLOMO: Ag shame! Maybe the poor boy was hungry.

STEWART: You can't eat that food. It is many years old.

PROFESSOR: I don't think he plans to eat it, Lord Stewart. I think he just wants to punish you for refusing to be part of his joke. He'll bring them back.

STEWART: I hope you're right, my dear Professor. Anyway, tomorrow I'm going to see the Virgin Mary in person rather than on toasted bread.

MADLOMO: After what I have seen and heard here I want to persuade that poor boy to come home with me.

PROFESSOR: You are serious about this, are you?

MADLOMO: It is the least that a woman can do. Save at least one child from the streets.

STEWART: You must be rich to want to adopt a big boy like that. Do you know how much he eats?

MADLOMO: Rich? What makes you think a poor woman who lives in a shack in Diepsloot is rich? It is *ubuntu* to save that child from the streets and from the likes of you.

STEWART: What will your husband and your family say about it when they see you out of the blue coming home with a boy you've picked up in the street?

MADLOMO: I don't have a husband. It's just me and my daughter, uBongi.

PROFESSOR: Bongi! I know Bongi. How is she?

MADLOMO [*agitated*]: How is she? You know very well how she is. She is sick with AIDS, that's how she is. You know very well what happened to her as a baby. People talked about it and made our lives difficult. And after the fire happened and my house was in cinders I had to run away to Johannesburg. They thought my child would die, but she's still here. She's still with me.

PROFESSOR: Oh, MaDlomo, I know the sad things that happened to you and the baby.

MADLOMO: Well, she's not a baby anymore. She is a big girl. The man who raped her when she was only three months old, thinking that she was curing his AIDS, died a long time ago. But *uBongi wami* is still alive. She's sick, yes, she's suffering, yes, but she's alive. And she is going to live and be a woman and have her own family.

She exits, still very disturbed.

STEWART: You knew about this?

PROFESSOR: Of course I know about it; we are from the same village, remember? I was still back there when it happened. I told you I used to drink at her shebeen. So, one night … it was a night I was not there … I am told that a man called her out to talk some business, or so he claimed. The baby was asleep on the bed, so maybe

MaDlomo thought she would just dash outside quickly and settle whatever business it was that the man wanted to discuss with her. It turned out that it was just a ruse. The man overpowered MaDlomo, tied her with ropes, and dumped her behind her rondavel. He then went into the house and raped the baby. MaDlomo was rescued many hours later – she couldn't scream because the man had stuffed rags in her mouth. When she got into the house the baby was a ruptured bloody mess. It had cried until it could not cry anymore. So it just lay there, on the verge of death.

STEWART [*visibly shaken*]: Why would anyone rape a three-month-old baby?

PROFESSOR: There is this stupid superstition doing the rounds that if you have AIDS and you have sex with a virgin you get cured. A baby possesses assured virginity.

STEWART: Holy Mary Mother of Jesus! Your people take the cake all the time! Black people never disappoint with their stupidity. I don't know how you got to be different, Professor.

PROFESSOR: It is very stupid. And very deadly. I didn't know MaDlomo's baby managed to survive. I'm glad she did. What broke the poor woman most was that while she was testing other people's daughters for virginity she couldn't save her own daughter.

STEWART: What foolish superstition!

PROFESSOR: You know, Lord Stewart, this whole myth of virgin cures is not new and did not start in South Africa. It was not invented by black people, either. We got it from Europe.

STEWART: You are joking, of course.

PROFESSOR: Not at all. It really was a white thing originally.

STEWART: Yeah, blame it on the white man, hey?

PROFESSOR: Black people adopted it because to them everything white is true and valid and worthy of adoption. The myth is centuries old.

STEWART: Aha! Now you get caught in your own false propaganda. There was no AIDS centuries ago.

PROFESSOR: It was about sexually transmitted infections of all types – especially syphilis. They believed it could be cured if one had sex with a virgin. No one knows where and when the myth started. It must have been around the sixteenth century, but it was widespread in parts of eastern Europe by the late eighteenth century and in Scotland in the nineteenth century. In Victorian England some men believed that they could cure their syphilis, which was fatal in those days, by having sex with virgins. There were even pseudo-scientists who explained how intact hymens and scanty vaginal secretions of virgins prevented the transmission of the disease.

STEWART: Proof! I want evidence of your slanderous pronouncements against my people, Professor.

PROFESSOR: It is not my people versus your people, Lord Stewart. It's just historical fact. I want you to read just one paragraph from the work of Hanne Blank.

He gets the book from the bench, pages through it and gives it to LORD STEWART.

STEWART: Who's Hanne Blank? One of your Black Power zealots who want to re-invent history?

PROFESSOR: She is a white woman; a virginity historian.

STEWART: Virginity has its own historians!

PROFESSOR: Come on, read. Just this one paragraph.

STEWART [*reading*]: 'Part of what is behind this practice is a
    naïve and hopeful belief in sympathetic magic. Across
    cultures and eras, virgins have been perceived as
    having a particular potent purity that acts as a shield
    and keeps the virgin from harm. In Christian virgin
    martyr legends, for instance, virgins often do battle
    with demons and with Satan himself while protected
    by virginity. Surely, the thinking goes, something
    powerful enough to vanquish demons can also cure
    syphilis. All one has to do is to take that something
    from the body of someone who still possesses it.'

PROFESSOR: Then she also tells us about a case of a 37-year-
    old coalminer in Glasgow in 1913 who was in court
    for raping his nine-year-old niece, infecting her
    with gonorrhoea and other venereal diseases. Dr
    James Devon gave evidence at the trial and, among
    other things, he said [*reading*]: 'There is a curiously
    persistent and widespread belief that a man who
    suffers from venereal disease can get rid of it by
    having connection with a virgin. I have been surprised
    at discovering the existence of this belief in people
    who are generally well informed as well as among the
    comparatively illiterate. I have tried to find evidence
    for the theory that it is a belief traceable to certain
    districts but I have discovered it among people of
    different places and of different occupations – so
    different that now I should scarcely be surprised to
    come across it anywhere.'

STEWART: This virginity thing is heavy, Professor. Very
    heavy.

PROFESSOR: You've said it before, Lord Stewart, and you're right.

STEWART: How did the myth of the virgin cures find its way to the Valley of a Thousand Hills so that a poor child, MaDlomo's three-month-old baby, was raped and savaged like that?

PROFESSOR: Remember we were colonised by people who believed in virgin cures.

STEWART: Aha! There we go again. Blame it on colonialism!

PROFESSOR: Black soldiers who returned to the Eastern Cape from the Second World War brought with them an outbreak of sexually transmitted infections. But they also brought back with them the virgin cure myth they had learnt in Europe. So it took root in the Eastern Cape and spread from there. Now, of course, today our charlatans remember how virgins were used to cure sexually transmitted infections and teach people that AIDS can be cured that way as well. Desperate people do desperate things.

STEWART: Desperate people do stupid things.

PROFESSOR: Today, virginity cure myths are flourishing not only in South Africa but also in such highly patriarchal societies as India and Thailand.

The SELLER OF LAUGHTER enters, singing and dancing. He is waving the slice of toast and the potato crisp as he kicks his legs towards LORD STEWART.

SELLER [*singing*]: You steal a man's mushrooms; he steals your bread and chip. You refuse to be his slave in chains; he eats your bread and chip ...

LORD STEWART tries to tackle him, but he ducks away and

skips around the playground equipment with STEWART chasing him.

STEWART: I'm going to kill you for this, you moron. And who says I stole your mushrooms?

The SELLER OF LAUGHTER pushes the merry-go-round and rides. LORD STEWART reaches for him.

SELLER: Who else can steal my mushrooms? The Professor is only interested in his stupid books that make him even more stupid. He can't be the one who stole my zoomers.

STEWART: Come on, man, give me my stuff. Those are holy relics. You don't know what they mean to me.

SELLER: Be my slave first, Lord Stewart. The Mother of All Jokes. Then I'll give you your stuff. You're lucky I didn't eat the bread. It's as hard as a brick.

STEWART: If anything happens to my sacred relics you'll be cursed forever!

SELLER: Be my slave, Lord Stewart! Be my slave!

He jumps off the merry-go-round, runs around the playground equipment with LORD STEWART after him, and they both exit.

Lights fade to black.

Act Two

Scene 1

Lights rise on the park. None of the denizens is there. MADLOMO enters. She is immediately followed by a wide-eyed THABISILE, who wanders in with trepidation. MADLOMO is not wearing her orange overalls today but is dressed in her Zulu traditional attire of an isidwaba *skirt made of faded black towelling, a black* isicholo *headdress and faded black sneakers with black socks. THABISILE is wearing a light blue, two-piece costume that makes her look like the primary school teacher she is.*

THABISILE: There's no one here.

MADLOMO: This is where he lives ... with a white man and a boy. But I've not seen the white man for days now. They say he went on a pilgrimage.

THABISILE: Okay, they're not here. Let's go.

MADLOMO: Not so fast! You need to face the past once and for all, Thabisile. Who knows, you may even be able to save him from his anger and bitterness.

THABISILE: How do you know he wants to see me?

MADLOMO: I heard him when he was talking about you. There was a softness in his voice when he mentioned your name.

THABISILE: I didn't think he would mention me. I didn't think he would remember me at all. It's been many years, MaDlomo.

MADLOMO: He needs you. All he does is sit here and read and talk a lot of *amampunge* about his own culture. Books have messed up his head. So have the white people who stay here with him.

THABISILE: He needs me? I needed him too, but that was a long time ago. Where was he when I needed him?

MADLOMO: He says you left him.

THABISILE: I left because he was not man enough to stand up for me. He knew the truth but he was silent. Then other things happened as well. He left. He's the one who left.

MADLOMO [*puzzled*]: You left, he left? Who left who exactly?

THABISILE: It's the past, MaDlomo. I don't want to bring that up. It is irrelevant. I've moved on. We've all moved on. I don't know why I agreed to come here.

MADLOMO: Because you still love him! I could see the excitement ... the expectation ... in your eyes when I told you I had discovered him. Listen, I must go to the demonstration at the court now.

THABISILE: I'm going with you.

MADLOMO: No, you stay here and wait for him. I'll come back to check on you.

THABISILE: Stay here on my own?

MADLOMO: Nothing will eat you, Thabisile. Wait for him here. It will be a wonderful surprise. Meeting you will bring him back into the fold of his people.

We can see that THABISILE does not think this is a good idea.
Nonetheless, she sits on the bench, albeit reluctantly.

MADLOMO: I'll be back very soon. When more women arrive
at the demonstration I'll be able to leave. Don't worry,
you'll be fine here.

She exits. THABISILE sits on the bench for a while, contemplating
her surroundings. She looks at the playground equipment and
then stands up and tries the swing. It sways for some time, then
she jumps down to the merry-go-round. She pushes it, then
rides on it. The SELLER OF LAUGHTER enters and is surprised
to see her. He watches for a while, but as soon as THABISILE
sees him she stops the merry-go-round.

THABISILE [*embarrassed*]: I was just thinking it would be
nice to have this in my schoolyard.

SELLER: You a teacher then?

THABISILE: Yes, at a primary school in Diepsloot.

SELLER: That's a depressing place, Diepsloot. I lived there
once, before I ran away from home. Now this is my
home. Isn't it beautiful, with all the flowers and the
lawn and the merry-go-round and the swing and the
see-saw?

THABISILE: But there's no roof. What do you do when it rains
or when it gets to be too cold? Winter is coming soon.

SELLER: Under the bridge or in store verandas. There is a guy
they call Professor here; sometimes he pays for us at
some hostel when he has the money. He's not a real
professor, though. They call him that because he always
comes back here with a whole bunch of books and sits
here and reads them and argues about a lot of crap.

THABISILE: You're the boy.

SELLER: I'm not a boy. I'm a man. [*Lasciviously*] And I can show you that I'm a man.

THABISILE: Okay, you're the man that MaDlomo told me about.

SELLER: Want me to show you that I'm a man?

THABISILE: You don't need to show me anything. I believe you.

SELLER: We can do it before the others come.

THABISILE begins to show some consternation.

> I know, I know, you are much older and all that. But I like older women. My first time was with a woman much older than you. Before my father's drunken violence against me and my mother drove me out of Diepsloot. She was my mother's friend and she taught me quite a few tricks.

THABISILE: You could easily be my own son, so stop entertaining such ideas.

SELLER: But I'm not, and it's just the two of us here.

She is no longer afraid. She has sized him up and surmised that he is harmless.

THABISILE [*firmly*]: Stop it!

SELLER: I hear you, you don't have to yell.

THABISILE [*sighing with relief*]: When are the others coming back?

SELLER: Who cares if they come back at all? Come let's do the see-saw.

He goes to the see-saw.

THABISILE: I don't play children's games.

SELLER: You don't play adults' games and you don't play
children's games?

THABISILE: I don't play any games, finish and klaar.

SELLER: But you were playing when I got here. Come on,
don't be such a party pooper. It will be fun. I like the
see-saw but I don't get to play on it because you can't
do it on your own. Lord Stewart is a swing man and
the Professor is a useless pumpkin that just sits on the
bench like a bag of potatoes for the rest of his life.

THABISILE joins him at the see-saw but is hesitant to get on it.

Come on ... don't be afraid ... you'll have fun ...
Promise.

THABISILE [*laughs as she gets on her side of the see-saw*]: I
hope you're still talking about the see-saw.

*They play on the see-saw. Soon they are giggling and then
laughing like two kids.*

SELLER: I'm glad you came. I never get to do this.

*PROFESSOR enters, pushing a supermarket trolley full of books
and sundry items typical of homelessness. He pays no attention
to the pair on the see-saw, but the SELLER OF LAUGHTER sees
him immediately he enters. THABISILE does not because she
has her eyes closed and is laughing away.*

SELLER: Hey Professor, eat your heart out, you old bastard!

*PROFESSOR looks up and sees THABISILE. He is not sure
whether or not his eyes are playing tricks on him. THABISILE
sees him and stops the see-saw immediately.*

PROFESSOR: Thabisile?

THABISILE: You didn't think you'd ever see me again?

SELLER: Come on, *ausi*. We're still playing. *Re ntse re bapala.*

THABISILE and PROFESSOR walk towards each other.

PROFESSOR: What brings you here?

SELLER: Why did you come back, you old bastard ... to mess up our game?

PROFESSOR: It is MaDlomo, is it not? It's MaDlomo who told you where to find me.

SELLER: You stay away from her. I found her first.

THABISILE: Yes, she came to my school and persuaded me to come.

PROFESSOR: To your school? What school?

THABISILE: The primary school where I teach.

SELLER: Come, *ausi*, this man is not worth your time.

PROFESSOR [*irritated, but determined to ignore SELLER*]: You became a teacher? Maybe it's good that things happened the way they did. You became your own person.

THABISILE: You can't absolve yourself that way. There is nothing good about what happened.

PROFESSOR: Good for you, I mean. You became a professional woman. I became nothing.

THABISILE: I suppose that should console me?

The SELLER OF LAUGHTER tries to pull THABISILE away by the hand.

SELLER: Come, *ausi,* I'll show you a few tricks on the merry-go-round.

THABISILE looks at PROFESSOR and then at SELLER and smiles. She seems to be enjoying the fact that PROFESSOR is annoyed by SELLER. She wants to humour SELLER.

THABISILE: Okay. Show me what a real man can do on the merry-go-round.

She gets on it and SELLER pushes it. When it's going at full speed he quickly steps onto it too.

PROFESSOR: This is ridiculous, Thabisile.

SELLER: Go away, Professor. She's mine; I found her first!

PROFESSOR reaches for the bar of the merry-go-round and holds it. It stops and this annoys SELLER no end. He stands there and sulks like a kid whose candy has been snatched by a bully.

SELLER: You party-pooping bastard! *Ke tla u fumana ka leleng la matsatsi.*

He exits in a huff.

THABISILE: Why did you do that to the child?

PROFESSOR: That's no child that. That's a demon.

THABISILE: Since when have you become a bully?

He tries to hold her hand but she pulls away.

I don't know why MaDlomo asked me to come here. But whatever the reason, it has nothing to do with holding hands.

PROFESSOR: I don't know either. She didn't tell me what she

was planning to do. But it gives me the opportunity to tell you how sorry I am.

THABISILE: I have long since healed, so it is fine. After I was ostracised I became a wanderer for a long time, until I found myself.

PROFESSOR: You know, Thabisile, if I had known things would turn out the way they did, I would have stained our bedding with the blood of a chicken.

THABISILE: And in that way you would have stood up to the elders of your family and your grandmothers and the village gossips?

PROFESSOR cannot answer this. He is saved by the arrival of LORD STEWART, who is wearing dark glasses and finding his way with a white cane. He is blind.

PROFESSOR: Lord Stewart, you have been gone for many days!

THABISILE: So, this is your white man that MaDlomo told me about? *Kade ng'cabanga ukuth' ukhuluma ngomuntu obhadlile.*

STEWART: Is that the first thing you notice about me, Professor, that I've been gone for days?

PROFESSOR: Well, I also notice that you have adopted a new style of begging, posing as a blind man.

STEWART: And what makes you think I am posing, Professor? What makes you think I am not blind?

He takes off his glasses.

Look into my eyes? What do you see? A man who can see?

PROFESSOR: I don't see any difference.

He waves his hand in front of LORD STEWART's face, but STEWART does not react. He can't see. PROFESSOR does it over and over again, closer to the eyes, with the same result.

You're blind, Lord Stewart! What happened?

THABISILE: Was he not blind before?

STEWART: Who is this one?

PROFESSOR: Thabisile, my wife.

THABISILE: I am not your wife.

STEWART: The one who didn't have a stain?

THABISILE: So, I'm news among the beggars of
        Johannesburg?

PROFESSOR: What happened, Lord Stewart? Did you see Our
        Lady of Benoni?

STEWART: I looked at the sun, Professor.

THABISILE: Why did he look at the sun?

STEWART: It was part of my pilgrimage. It was wonderful in
        Benoni, Professor. I was one of hundreds of pilgrims
        who met Francesca Zackey and her mother, Bridgette.
        When my turn came I was welcomed right there in
        their living room. Francesca spoke in tongues, which
        could only be understood by her mother and other
        members of the family. She gave me a glass of water
        from the tap to drink. I tell you, Professor, the water
        supply at that home has turned into holy oil. I could
        taste the oil. Almost like extra virgin olive oil.

PROFESSOR: A miracle.

THABISILE: A miracle?

STEWART: Before my very eyes, my dear Professor. When Francesca touched me I just became jelly, as if I didn't have any bones in my body. I fell on my knees and was transported into another world.

PROFESSOR: Did you see Danni in that world?

STEWART: I didn't see anybody. I was dazed. When I came to my senses I was enveloped by peace and calm. She made a sign of the cross with the holy water on my forehead. All that time Francesca was speaking in tongues, asking the evil spirits to vacate my body and her father, Frank Zackey, was pacing the floor egging her on, encouraging the stubborn spirits to cooperate and hit the road. The walls in the room were covered with pictures of the Virgin Mary and her son.

THABISILE: These people prayed for you so hard that you got blind?

STEWART: She is of little faith, your wife.

THABISILE: I told you I'm not his wife. He missed the boat many years ago.

STEWART: Then it was time for the spinning sun. According to Francesca the sun has been spinning at sunset since the miracles of Benoni started. Hundreds of people have looked into the sun and have seen it spin. 'Look into the sun!' she commanded. I stared into it. 'Do you see colours of the rainbow pouring out of the sun? Look inside the giant fireball; there is the Virgin Mary, Our Lady of the Ray, placing a protective shield over it so that you may see her in all her glory! There is the Virgin Mary, behold the Virgin Mary!' I couldn't see anything. Just the blaze. The sun was burning my eyes. I screamed, but stubbornly looked. I came all the way to Benoni to see the Virgin. I wasn't going back without seeing her. I wanted to ask her to lead me to Danni. Or better still, to lead Danni back to me. I fell on the floor mumbling in pain. The Zackey family praised me for talking in tongues. I was a success story. I must have seen the Virgin, and she made me talk in tongues. I sat on the stoep for many hours, long after the pilgrims had left. I couldn't see. I thought my sight would come back and I sat there. Frank Zackey came and told me it was time to go. I told him I couldn't see, I was blind. He called Francesca and I asked her what would become of me. 'You asked me to look at the sun and I did. Now I can't see. What should I do?' She told me: 'It is out of my hands. People look at the sun at their own risk. I am not the sun.'

PROFESSOR: She's not the sun.

THABISILE: Look on the bright side.

STEWART: I looked on the bright side, that's why I'm blind.

THABISILE: At least blindness won't affect your job. You may even make more money as a genuinely blind beggar.

PROFESSOR: Do you think that's comforting to him?

STEWART: Danni! It was for Danni that I got to be like this.

PROFESSOR: She will be proud of you when she gets to hear that you went blind for her sake.

STEWART: How's she going to hear of it? I didn't see Our Lady of Benoni. Danni will never come back.

PROFESSOR: You never know, Lord Stewart. People have a way of coming back. Look at Thabisile, she came back.

STEWART: Your stainless wife.

THABISILE: I am not his wife and I have not come back.

STEWART: Well, you're here, aren't you? Danni will be here
      too one day. You're going to meet Danni, my dear
      Professor, and see what a lady she is. There was
      rhythm between us. Sometimes we would just sit on a
      park bench quietly and listen to each other's rhythm.
      But sometimes she annoyed me. Now that she's gone
      I regret that I got annoyed. I used to resent that I no
      longer had any privacy. She even wanted to know
      my thoughts. If I sat quietly she would ask: 'What
      are you thinking about?' Come on, now, can't a man
      have domain over his own thoughts? I dreaded that
      question. 'What are you thinking about?' 'Nothing,'
      I would say. 'My mind is a blank slate. You can write
      whatever thoughts you want it to have.' I thought that
      would be enough. But no! After a while she would ask
      again: 'What are you thinking about?'

*A jubilant MADLOMO enters. She is holding a placard
proclaiming: 'DEATH TO THE BITCH' and is* toyi-toying.

MADLOMO [*chanting*]: *Mayif'iBitch, if'iBitch! Bulal'iBitch,
      if'iBitch*!

*She does one or two rounds among the playground equipment.
THABISILE, amused by her antics, laughs and claps her hands.*

STEWART: Are we being invaded by the trade union people?

MADLOMO comes to a halt in front of them.

PROFESSOR [*to THABISILE*]: When you're encouraging her
      like this do you know who this bitch they want to kill
      is? The accuser of the Right Reverend Chief Comrade
      my Leader.

THABISILE: Come on, they're just talking. MaDlomo cannot
      kill anybody.

STEWART [*as if lost in his own world*]: You know, parks like these used to be very peaceful. In the good old days they used to be very quiet and peaceful.

PROFESSOR: You cannot chant that someone should be killed if it is not your intention to get her killed.

MADLOMO: You should be singing the praises of the Right Reverend Comrade my Leader instead of supporting those who falsely accuse him of a crime. Not only is he a good pastor of the church, with compassion and charitable works, he is a political leader who is on the side of the poor ... unlike those who are in power today.

PROFESSOR: The Right Reverend Comrade my Leader is a politician like all others. I stay away from lionising politicians because by nature I'm not a praise singer. In my experience there is not a single successful politician who has an ounce of integrity. Those who have integrity fail as politicians. That's the nature of the beast.

STEWART: No, it was not quiet. It was peaceful, but not quiet. There was the laughter of children and the chirping of the birds. The nannies sat on the grass – not on the benches; no black nanny could sit on the benches. They sat on the grass and gossiped about their madams while watching the kids play. You wouldn't have been allowed in this park, Professor. None of you would sit on these benches.

THABISILE: It is just a manner of speaking when she says 'kill the bitch'.

PROFESSOR: The other day she was defending the honour killings of girls, who are found not to be virgins, that happens in other countries.

MADLOMO: *Yini uqamb'amanga ngami manje*? Have you ever seen any honour killing in South Africa? I merely said to you virginity is so important that in other cultures people die for it. In our culture no one was ever killed for failing a virginity test. I would be the first one to condemn it if anything like that ever happened.

THABISILE: Non-virgins are not killed. They are just ostracised until they leave the village. *uBaba uMadonsela* left the village with the rest of his family because he refused to allow his daughter to attend virginity testing ceremonies. The chief banished them.

STEWART: I was one of those kids, you know, who played in a park like this. It could even have been this very park. My favourite was the swing. My nanny used to push me on the swing. I've always loved the swing.

MADLOMO: Whose side are you on *na kanti*, Thabisile.

PROFESSOR: She is on her own side. She herself was ostracised.

MADLOMO: Thabisile never failed my tests. No girl who failed any of my tests was ever ostracised. These tests are voluntary. Girls go there willingly and enjoy the festivities and the ceremonies. Were you ever forced, Thabisile?

THABISILE: Not directly. But other girls spoke ill of you when you didn't attend the virginity test ceremonies. They called you names, and didn't want to associate with you. If you wanted to live happily in the village you'd be a fool not to go. I attended voluntarily myself, but some of my friends' parents forced them to attend.

PROFESSOR: And yet you failed the final test, after passing all of MaDlomo's tests. You see what I mean?

STEWART: The ice cream van used to come by and stop at the gate of the park. Our moms gave our nannies money to buy us ice cream. So when the van came by we all ran to the gate to choose the suckers we wanted. I didn't like the red ones. I liked green. It tasted like lime. Or blue. Blue was always good. It left your tongue looking nice and blue.

MADLOMO [to PROFESSOR]: What's wrong with your white man?

PROFESSOR: He'll be fine once he gets used to his blindness.

MADLOMO: He's playing blind? You beggars are a bunch of crooks.

THABISILE: *Uyamkhumbula mos uBab'uMkhonza?*

PROFESSOR: Yes, I do remember Mkhonza. He was the richest man in the village. He owned the general dealer store where we sold corn and beans from our fields after harvest and the skins of our animals when we had slaughtered for the ancestors.

THABISILE: He sent his daughter to doctors in Cape Town to reconstruct her girlhood so she could pass the test. And she did.

MADLOMO: There is nothing like that. There is no doctor who can bring back virginity once it's lost.

PROFESSOR: Oh, yes, doctors do that all the time. It's called hymenoplasty – hymen reconstruction surgery. It doesn't bring back virginity because virginity does not exist. So, the old man paid thousands of rands to fool MaDlomo?

THABISILE: The aim was not to fool anyone. All he wanted was to save his daughter from shame and ridicule.

MADLOMO: No one could fool me. I used to have other tests too, besides examining the girls' private parts.

THABISILE: The pencil test! I remember the pencil test!

MADLOMO: Shhhh ... Don't tell this man our secrets *wena*.

LORD STEWART feels the path with his cane, fumbling now and then, until he finds the swing. He gets on it and begins to sway gently.

> *Umlungu wakho* really takes his blindness seriously.

PROFESSOR: You would too if you were blind. The pencil test? Just like in the days of apartheid. They used to put a pencil in your hair and if it stayed then you were declared a Bantu. Many coloured folks lost their privileged status and became natives after failing the pencil test.

THABISILE: MaDlomo's test was similar to that. She put a pencil under a girl's breast. If it fell the girl was a virgin and if it stayed she was no longer a virgin.

MADLOMO: It is the wisdom of the ages; it is the wisdom of our ancestors.

PROFESSOR: Maybe your ancestors were European, because that's where the pencil test comes from.

STEWART: Professor knows a lot about things that come from Europe. He told us about virgin cures. Will virginity cure my blindness, Professor? Will it?

PROFESSOR: I told you about Hanne Blank's investigations into the matter. Let me read again what she writes about the pencil test. [*He pages through a book and reads.*] 'Women's magazines in the mid-twentieth century advised readers to assess the pertness of their breasts by seeing whether the breast sagged sufficiently to hold a pencil in place against the rib cage. Only those whose breasts could not keep the pencil from falling passed this test.' And all this time MaDlomo thought her ancestors invented the pencil test!

MADLOMO: Just because white people used it doesn't mean our people didn't think of it too. Every Zulu woman knows that a virgin's breasts must be small and plump. Immediately they sag, with nipples pointing to the ground we know the girl is no longer a virgin.

PROFESSOR: I've said it before: virginity testing is nothing but physical assault on innocent girls. It is child abuse!

THABISILE: And there was another one. Another test, called *ukushikila*.

MADLOMO: Thabisile! *Yini ngawe kanti?*

THABISILE: We lifted our skirts and opened our legs to be inspected for the firmness of our breasts and the muscle tone of our private parts.

She is all giggly as she demonstrates ukushikila, *to MADLOMO's consternation.*

MADLOMO: You have no shame, Thabisile, to reveal the secrets of womanhood.

PROFESSOR: I know about these things, MaDlomo. Why do you think I condemn them? I went out of my way to find out about them.

MADLOMO: It worked for us. You may laugh at it but it worked all the time. Girls who were found not to be virgins through the pencil test admitted that they had indeed engaged in some dirty business with boys. Just like the Reed Dance test. It works!

THABISILE: Ah! The Reed Dance! I attended the very first
Reed Dance, in 1984.

PROFESSOR: You see what I meant *ke*, MaDlomo? The first
Reed Dance was in 1984, and you call it our culture?
You guys just copied the thing from Swaziland.

MADLOMO: The King brought it back in order to stop teenage
pregnancy, so it is our culture again now.

THABISILE: We went to get the reeds for the King. Hundred
of girls singing and laughing and dancing. Only the
girls who were virgins were allowed to carry the reeds.
If a non-virgin carried the reed it withered, showing
that the girl was no longer complete. It was a disgrace
if your reed withered; you would be removed from
the company of other girls. During the dance we were
required to show our breasts, abdomen and buttocks.
[*She giggles girlishly.*] My reeds never withered.

PROFESSOR: Another example of passing the test only to fail
the ultimate one.

MADLOMO: What are we standing here for, talking women's
things with this man? I promised I'd come back for you.

THABISILE: Yes, it is time to leave.

PROFESSOR: Are you going to come again?

THABISILE: What for?

PROFESSOR: Just to talk about old times.

THABISILE: There is nothing interesting about the old times,
Professor, as your fellow beggars call you.

PROFESSOR: I do not beg, Thabisile. I may live with them here
but I'm not a beggar.

MADLOMO: Let's go, Thabisile.

PROFESSOR: Let's go, Thabisile? Why did you bring her here then?

THABISILE: Let's go, MaDlomo.

They exit.

PROFESSOR: Can you believe that?

STEWART: Are they gone? Are the prattling women gone?

PROFESSOR: They are gone.

STEWART: Peace at last.

The SELLER OF LAUGHTER enters with a bouquet of flowers.

PROFESSOR: You spoke too soon.

STEWART: Are they back?

PROFESSOR: It is the Seller of Laughter.

SELLER: Where is *ausi*? I brought her flowers. She's a teacher, you know? She can help me compose the Mother of All Jokes.

He sees LORD STEWART.

> Ha! Lord Stewart! I see you're playing a blind man. You're not going to make more money that way. No one gives a damn for the blind.

STEWART: Can't you see? I am bloody blind!

SELLER: Oh, yeah? Then I am bloody deaf and mute and crippled from the waist down. Where is *ausi*?

His eyes search around, but THABISILE is not there.

SELLER [*to PROFESSOR*]: What did you do to her, you old
bastard?

Lights fade to black.

Scene 2

Lights rise on the SELLER OF LAUGHTER and THABISILE. They are playing on the see-saw and singing a child-like song. It is a Sunday and THABISILE is wearing jeans. There is a big birthday cake on the bench.

THABISILE [*singing*]: We go ...

SELLER [*singing*]: Up ...

THABISILE: And down ...

SELLER: And up ...

THABISILE: And down ...

SELLER: Okay! Okay!

He stops the see-saw.

      Let's go and eat the cake.

THABISILE: No, we must wait for the others ... for Professor.

SELLER: What do you care about him? He's not here.

THABISILE: I baked it for him.

SELLER: For him? What for? I heard he is the guy who treated you so bad. I wouldn't treat you bad if you were my wife.

THABISILE: Thank you. I don't think he meant to treat me badly at all. It was just the place and the times. You wouldn't understand.

SELLER: And so you bake *him* a cake?

THABISILE: It's his birthday.

SELLER: He never said anything about a birthday.

THABISILE: Maybe he forgot. I just wanted to surprise him, that's all.

SELLER: What about me?

THABISILE: I'll bake you one when it's your birthday too. When is your birthday?

SELLER: Well, I don't know. I think it is today. Yes, today's my birthday too.

THABISILE [*humouring him*]: Okay, it's your birthday too. We are celebrating two birthdays.

SELLER: So, can I have my share of the birthday before he comes back?

THABISILE: Just a small slice.

She cuts him a slice of the cake.

SELLER [*singing*]: 'Go Seller, it's a birthday, you gonna party like it's your birthday.'

He dances a clownish jig and THABISILE joins him. They hold each other's hands as they kick their legs in a silly dance. PROFESSOR enters, guiding LORD STEWART. PROFESSOR is carrying newspapers under one arm. THABISILE suddenly stops, obviously embarrassed that she has been caught in such childish jinks.

PROFESSOR: What are you doing with that boy?

SELLER: I'm not a boy; I'm a man.

THABISILE: We are celebrating your birthday.

SELLER: My birthday too.

STEWART: It's your birthday, Professor, and you said nothing about it.

SELLER: My birthday too, Lord Stewart.

PROFESSOR: I don't remember a damn thing about it. Who can remember birthdays in a place like this?

STEWART: Well, she remembered it. Your wife remembered it.

THABISILE: I am not his wife!

STEWART: Are you letting a small matter of a stain come between you?

PROFESSOR: Well, I'll be damned! It's my birthday and I didn't know a damn thing about it.

SELLER: And yet you're supposed to be the clever one. I've always known that it's my birthday today.

STEWART: Happy birthday, Seller of Laughter! Happy birthday, my dear Professor.

PROFESSOR leads LORD STEWART to his swing where he sways gently, then he places the newspapers on the bench next to the cake.

SELLER: You from the traffic lights, Lord Stewart? With him?

STEWART: No. He took me to the government offices to apply for a disability grant for my blindness.

THABISILE: On a Sunday?

PROFESSOR: We forgot it was Sunday. I don't keep track of the days of the week.

SELLER: You should have asked me. I knew it was a Sunday. That's why I have taken a day off.

THABISILE: Okay, let's have some cake.

SELLER: Where is the candle? I want to make a wish.

THABISILE: Oh, man! I forgot about the candles! We'll just imagine them and you can make a wish secretly in your heart.

She cuts the cake and serves each of them a piece on a paper serviette.

SELLER: My wish is not secret. I want Lord Stewart to be my slave in the Mother of All Jokes. That's my wish.

STEWART: In your dreams.

PROFESSOR: You are blind now, Lord Stewart. What choice do you have? It may serve you well to have a guide when you beg at the traffic lights.

SELLER: Yes, the Professor is not stupid all the time. And if I am going to be your guide at all there must be something in it for me. *Ha ke sebeletsi mahala nna.*

THABISILE [*singing*]: 'Happy birthday to you all ...'

PROFESSOR: I'd have bought some wine if I'd known it was my birthday.

THABISILE [*singing*]: 'It's your birthday, happy birthday ...'

The rest join in the song, as they chew the cake.

ALL [*singing*]: 'It's your birthday, happy birthday to you ...'

SELLER [*singing*]: 'Happy birthday to me ...'

THABISILE: MaDlomo should have been here too. *Phela ngumkhay'uMaDlomo.*

STEWART: I should have known it's Sunday. The prattling
　　　　virginity tester is not here today.

SELLER: MaDlomo is a nice lady. It's Professor who provokes
　　　　her.

PROFESSOR: As far as you're concerned there is never ever
　　　　anything that is right with me, *wena* Seller of Laughter.

THABISILE: The Seller of Laughter is right.

PROFESSOR: When he says I provoke MaDlomo?

SELLER [*beaming*]: You see? I am right.

THABISILE: You must give her a break. She means well. She
　　　　is fighting AIDS with her virginity tests.

PROFESSOR: Throughout the Valley of a Thousand Hills
　　　　where virginity tests have been going on since the
　　　　1980s people still die of AIDS. Our province has a
　　　　higher rate of infections than any other province.

SELLER: Are you blaming that on MaDlomo?

THABISILE: Is it MaDlomo's fault?

STEWART: Professor is just saying the provinces with the
　　　　lowest incidence of HIV/AIDS don't practise any of your
　　　　virginity testing *manga-manga* as part of their culture.
　　　　Therefore virginity tests don't prevent AIDS.

PROFESSOR: And the province that continues to wage war on
　　　　women with virginity tests ...

THABISILE: They say they test boys too these days.

PROFESSOR: I know, I know, in order to hide the fact of
　　　　misogyny there's a lie that boys are tested too. How
　　　　the hell do you test a boy? You can't hide the fact that

the problem of virginity is the problem of patriarchy. But what I am trying to point out is that our province, which prides itself in its culture of virginity tests, continues to have the highest rates of infections. Clearly your virginity tests and your Reed Dances are not helping the situation. Swaziland with its Reed Dance has the highest per capita HIV infections of all the countries in Africa.

SELLER: Per capita? What the fuck is capita?

PROFESSOR [*losing all patience with SELLER*]: I've had enough of your crap, *wena*.

THABISILE: *Hayibo*! Are you going to bully the child now?

SELLER: It is capital! The capital of Swaziland is Mbabane. You didn't think I know that?

PROFESSOR: I'll throw you out of here if you keep on getting on my nerves.

THABISILE: I hope you don't think I'm a defender of virginity testing.

PROFESSOR: I hope not. You and I are victims of the culture of virginity.

THABISILE: I am just saying also look at things from their point of view. Have some tolerance.

PROFESSOR: Do you know why we have higher rates of HIV than anywhere else? I think some of these infections are caused by virginity testing.

THABISILE: What evidence do you have of that?

PROFESSOR: I don't have any evidence of that. It's a reasonable assumption, though. What qualifications do MaDlomo or any of those women have, besides being active in local party politics? Have they studied anatomy? I heard that they don't even use gloves when they mess around with the private parts of hundreds of girls – one after the other. Is it true?

STEWART: Calm down, Professor, it's your birthday.

SELLER [*sulkily*]: I want more cake.

THABISILE: They only use gloves for overweight girls.

PROFESSOR: The logic being?

THABISILE: They say it is not easy to ascertain virginity without using the bare fingers when touching the girls' labia. But with fat girls gloves don't interfere.

PROFESSOR: Why do I suspect that *ooMaDlomo* are enjoying their job? Are they not getting some thrill from fiddling with the vaginas of little girls?

THABISILE: I think you are maligning these women.

PROFESSOR: I've said it before: virginity testing itself is child sexual abuse! It is even worse that *ooMaDlomo* do it in public, in community halls and open fields. *Yizingane zabantu lezi* who are being subjected to such humiliation.

SELLER [*yelling*]: I want more cake.

PROFESSOR [*yelling back*]: Just eat the damn cake, man. Eat all of it until you choke or throw up. Just eat the damn cake and get out of here.

STEWART: Just leave it to the government, my dear Professor. If, as you say, this is bad and terrible and abusive, then for sure the government must ban it.

The SELLER OF LAUGHTER has no laughter in him. He is angry. He goes for the cake and stuffs himself, while paging through Professor's newspapers.

PROFESSOR: I don't think the government has the balls to take that step. They don't want to alienate an important constituency like that. It's all politics.

THABISILE: The government would have to deal with circumcision in the Eastern Cape first, where boys actually die or are maimed for life. But they won't touch circumcision because it is a Xhosa thing. I haven't heard of anyone dying of virginity testing.

PROFESSOR: And you say you are not a defender of virginity testing? I am saying virginity testing, by its very nature, is a misogynistic act. It promotes negative patriarchal values – women's virginity is a prize that must be preserved for the benefit of men.

STEWART: Professor! Professor! It is women who force virginity testing on other women! Why should it be the man who is to blame?

PROFESSOR: They enforce it on behalf of men. Like in the days of apartheid. Your people, Lord Stewart, enforced those racist laws through my people. When there was no stain, Thabisile ...

THABISILE: Like you have broadcast that already in all the parks of Johannesburg.

PROFESSOR: When there was no stain you had offended the patriarchs: your father, your father-in-law and, supposedly, me. The womenfolk – your mother-in-law, my busybody grandmothers had to exact the punishment on our behalf.

PROFESSOR notices SELLER reading his newspaper. Angrily he snatches the paper away.

You know I hate it when someone reads my papers before I do.

THABISILE [*laughs*]: You're still like that?

SELLER: It's only a newspaper, you old bastard.

THABISILE: You always hated it when someone opened your newspaper before you did, even if they left it exactly as it was before.

LORD STEWART bursts out laughing. They all stop and look at him.

STEWART: You see, Professor, you also have the virginity mentality. You have read all these books that have made you aware, but your brain still remains a male brain. Your newspaper has to be a virgin paper. You must be the first to get between its pages. Like the patriarchs of the Valley of a Thousand Hills you have the virginity mentality!

PROFESSOR: That's a stretch, Lord Stewart.

SELLER: That's what I said; it is only a newspaper.

STEWART: What do you get when you read a newspaper that has not been read by anyone before you? It's still the same newspaper with the same news.

SELLER: Yes, I am not going to eat the damn paper. I just wanted to see if I could get some ideas for my joke, that's all.

THABISILE: Exactly, Lord Stewart. What does a man get when he sleeps with a virgin?

PROFESSOR: Besides the annoying lack of experience? Nothing, but the ego that he was the first, and is the sole owner of this female body and its creative power.

STEWART: Perhaps he may even think that the creative force will be transferred to him with all its mysteries. What could be more mysterious than virginity?

THABISILE: *Uyabona ke manje lapho*, I hate it when you men start romanticising about the female body like that.

STEWART [*laughing*]: He is confessing to his virginity mentality, madam.

PROFESSOR: He can read the damn paper for all I care!

He throws the newspaper to the SELLER OF LAUGHTER, who ducks instead of catching it.

SELLER: I don't want your stupid paper. Thabisile will help me create my joke.

THABISILE: You tell me what it is all about and I'll help you.

THABISILE and the SELLER OF LAUGHTER walk to where he keeps his boards. He shows her some of the signs. We don't hear what they are saying, but from their laughter it is obvious that they are having fun. She either thinks the signs are funny or she is just playing along to humour him. PROFESSOR sits on the bench and reads a newspaper, every now and again stealing a glance at the pair. His gaze is disapproving.

STEWART: So, my dear Professor, now that you have found her what are you going to do with her?

PROFESSOR: I didn't find her, Lord Stewart. MaDlomo brought her here.

STEWART: After that she came on her own, bringing you a cake. Methinks your penitence has come to an end.

Whatever wrong you did, I think she has forgiven you. Seize the moment, my dear Professor.

PROFESSOR: When did you become a wise man all of a sudden?

STEWART: Since I went blind. You become a sage with blindness. You told me that you were a penitent. I am saying that your penitence seems to have come to an end. Your worries are over.

PROFESSOR: Maybe you're right. Oh, how I wish you were right. What about yours, Lord Stewart. I worry about you. How are you going to make it at the traffic lights?

STEWART: You think my sight is gone forever?

PROFESSOR: We don't know. But in the meantime you need to earn a living. You cannot do it without a guide. And if Thabisile and me, if we get together again, I won't be staying here to help you.

STEWART: I'll have to manage somehow. I am an old seadog, Professor.

PROFESSOR: The Seller of Laughter can be very useful to you, you know. Participate in his joke and be his slave. You'll earn a lot of money together. As his slave you'll be his meal ticket and he'll be your guide. It's worth thinking about.

STEWART: Yeah, it is worth thinking about. But I tell you I'll be back in Benoni for more blessings. My sight will return. So will Danni. I don't lose hope, my dear Professor.

They are quiet for a while as PROFESSOR reads the paper. There is an occasional giggle from the other couple. Then PROFESSOR sees something in the paper which excites him.

PROFESSOR: Hey, Lord Stewart, I think the game is up for Francesca Zackey.

STEWART: What do you mean the game is up for Francesca Zackey? She's not involved in any game.

PROFESSOR: You can kiss Our Lady of Benoni goodbye – the church is shutting down her operation.

STEWART: You call it 'operation' as if she was involved in some scam. If only you had made the pilgrimage, Professor, you'd have been overwhelmed by the sacredness of it all.

PROFESSOR: Okay, listen. [*He reads.*] 'The Catholic Church has told Benoni teenager Francesca Zackey to stop blessing pilgrims after some pilgrims severely damaged their eyes. Yesterday, the Southern African Catholic Bishops' Conference, the highest Catholic authority in the region, asked Francesca not to receive pilgrims, speak to the media or encourage people to look into the sun. "We would consider it better if she took time off to think about what has happened."'

STEWART: Who the blazes do they think they are to stop the blessings? This means I'll never get to see Our Lady of Benoni.

PROFESSOR: You're blind, Lord Stewart. You can't see Our Lady of Benoni in any case.

STEWART: I was going to regain my sight. I was going to see the Holy Virgin. She was going to return my Danni to me. How can they stop the blessings before I regain my sight?

LORD STEWART is really upset. He stumbles away from the swing and almost falls. PROFESSOR comes to his aid and helps him up. The SELLER OF LAUGHTER comes running to help. So does THABISILE.

SELLER [*accusingly*]: What did you do to him?

PROFESSOR: Did you see me do anything to him?

SELLER: You must have said something. What did he tell you, Lord Stewart?

STEWART: That I'll be blind forever.

THABISILE: How can you say such a cruel thing to a blind man?

PROFESSOR: It's the church, not me. They've stopped the blessings.

STEWART: Take me for a walk. I need some fresh air.

PROFESSOR: Hey, we are in an open park here, Lord Stewart. There's plenty of fresh air.

THABISILE: Take him for a walk.

SELLER: I'll take you for a walk, Lord Stewart.

The SELLER OF LAUGHTER guides LORD STEWART towards the exit. But before they leave he turns and faces PROFESSOR menacingly.

You old bastard!

They exit.

PROFESSOR: I disapprove of you cavorting with this boy.

THABISILE: *You* disapprove? You talk like a man who has managed to liberate himself from the values of the elders of your clan, but deep down you are still in bondage; you are a Zuluboy who thinks you own a woman and you can therefore approve or disapprove of her behaviour.

PROFESSOR: *Wenza ukuthi angidelele mos.*

THABISILE: *Kade ekudelela* even before I came here. It is how you relate to each other as beggars.

PROFESSOR: I told you, I'm not a beggar.

THABISILE: Then what are you doing here?

PROFESSOR: What else could I do after all that happened to us? After you left I was completely broken.

THABISILE: It's more than that, isn't it? You could have moved on as I did, you were strong enough to do so. But other things overtook you, didn't they?

PROFESSOR: You know about it?

THABISILE: I spoke to your brother at Addington Hospital in Durban. He sent for me when he didn't have long to live and told me everything.

PROFESSOR: *Nkulunkulu wami*! What did Duma tell you?

THABISILE: Everything. He wanted to talk to you but no one knew where you were. You had just disappeared. So he sent for me and told me everything. Men tell the truth when they are getting ready to meet their maker. He was guilty that you went through all that for him.

PROFESSOR [*urgently*]: I want you back, Thabisile. We still have a chance.

THABISILE: What makes you think I have just been sitting there waiting for you? What makes you take it for granted that there is no man in my life?

PROFESSOR: Is there?

THABISILE: No. But I cannot take you back until you make things right with MaDlomo.

PROFESSOR: It is a difficult thing you're asking me to do, Thabisile.

THABISILE: Only if you come clean with MaDlomo and she forgives you will I forgive you.

PROFESSOR: We must let sleeping dogs lie, Thabisile.

THABISILE: Obviously they are not sleeping or you would not be wasting away in a park in Johannesburg. They are barking so loudly that we can hear them all the way from KwaVimba in the Valley of a Thousand Hills.

PROFESSOR: MaDlomo is not innocent either. Nobody is asking her to come and account to those she wronged, the little lives she ruined. Why should I account to her?

THABISILE: You don't have to. But I cannot be part of your life if you don't. I cannot be with you while you carry this burden on your conscience, for I would have to share it with you. I am not prepared to do that. It took me a long time to be free. I cannot go back to bondage again. You free yourself first, and then you may come to me. We can only meet on equal terms as two free people.

PROFESSOR is crestfallen. THABISILE exits.

Lights fade to black.

Scene 3

Lights rise on PROFESSOR. He is sorting out his worldly possessions, which include a few clothes, a blanket, newspapers and lots of books, and packing them into a supermarket trolley. An ebullient MADLOMO enters, dressed in her orange overalls and carrying a sign with the message: VICTORY TO THE PEOPLE. She is singing and dancing, obviously the remnants of a song from her demonstration. She gets to the bench and dances around PROFESSOR. He ignores her and continues with his work.

MADLOMO: We won. The women of South Africa have won. The ancestors heard our call and answered it positively.

PROFESSOR: Congratulations on your victory. I am leaving. I'm relocating to another place where the likes of you will never find me again.

MADLOMO: *Wathint'abafazi*!

PROFESSOR: I curse the day you came to work here.

MADLOMO: There is nothing that you can say that will dampen my spirits. Nothing in the world can spoil my day today. Come on; tell me any nonsense you like about virginity testing and all your other silly complaints and see if I care. Today is a wonderful day ... a wonderful week ... a great year. We were vindicated. The verdict came. The Right Reverend Comrade Chief my Leader was found not guilty. It was

consensual sex, the wise judges decided. The bitch has
run away and is now in hiding.

PROFESSOR: After she was threatened with death ...

MADLOMO: Don't you understand? It was political. She
was planted by his political enemies. She seduced
him in order to cry rape. She didn't reckon with us.
Wathint'abafazi! You strike a woman, you strike a rock.

PROFESSOR: What was he doing, he who has posed as a moral
leader, allowing himself to be seduced?

MADLOMO: The Right Reverend Chief Comrade my Leader is
a man of God first and foremost. What belongs to God
belongs to him. He takes. That's what he does. He takes
what he is entitled to. *Adle kuphi umelusi? Umelusi udla
emhlambini.* A shepherd eats from his own flock.

PROFESSOR: Let them eat, MaDlomo. *Ngiyahamba mina.*

MADLOMO: Where to? *Uyakuphi kanti manje?*

PROFESSOR: I do not know where I will end up. But it must be
far from you or from anyone else from KwaVimba.

MADLOMO: How will Thabisile find you? Does she even know
that you are running away from her again?

PROFESSOR: I don't want her to find me.

MADLOMO: You coward! Not after I went to all the trouble of
finding her for you.

PROFESSOR: You should have just left things the way they
were. I just wanted things to stay the way they were.

MADLOMO: I think she still loves you, you know.

PROFESSOR: Is that what she told you?

MADLOMO: I cannot tell you what she told me. But take it from me, she still has strong feelings for you.

PROFESSOR: That's why I must go.

MADLOMO: Running away again? Because you know you have remained nothing while she has made something of herself? You are running away from yourself, but you'll always be there. You can't outrun yourself.

PROFESSOR: It's not that.

MADLOMO: It can only be that. You feel like a castrated man in her presence.

PROFESSOR: I am not running away from Thabisile.

MADLOMO: Then I am right; you are running away from yourself.

PROFESSOR [*frantic*]: I tell you I am not. I was happy until you came here.

MADLOMO: You can't get very far running away from yourself.

PROFESSOR: I am running away from you.

MADLOMO: I know you hate me for being true to my culture of virginity testing. But you don't have to vacate your park on my account. They tell me you have lived here for years. I am only here for an hour a day at the most. I clean other parks in town too. [*Laughs*] Whatever park you choose for your new home, if it is in this city I'll be there too one day. It just depends where the municipality sends me.

PROFESSOR: It has nothing to do with your virginity testing, MaDlomo, though I find it reprehensible. It is Thabisile.

MADLOMO: Coward! *Hamba gwala ndini*!

PROFESSOR: She won't have me back until I tell you the truth.

MADLOMO's expression shows that she does not understand.

> The truth about things that made you leave
> KwaVimba.

MADLOMO: I don't need to be told by you why I left Kwa-
Vimba. Everyone knows that I left because my baby
was raped. My three-month-old baby. And when I took
her to the clinic my house was set on fire. Everything I
owned was destroyed. Relatives gave me shelter while
we waited for the police to come from Pietermaritzburg
to investigate. The elders of the village and the chief
wanted me to keep quiet about what had happened
for the sake of community cohesion. My baby was
raped, my house set on fire, yet they wanted me to be
strong and bear it like a woman. The man was caught
and he only got a one-year sentence. In the meantime
my enemies were laughing at me – those who had
been against our virginity testing ceremonies were
saying: 'It serves MaDlomo right; the famous virginity
tester is now stuck with a girl child who is no longer
a virgin.' I couldn't live with that shame. I escaped to
Johannesburg. I was fearful that they would come back
and burn my shelter again.

PROFESSOR: No, they would not come back and burn your
shelter again. They had also left. They had also escaped
to Johannesburg.

MADLOMO: You know who they are? They were never caught.
The rapist denied that he did it.

PROFESSOR: The rapist did not do it. I did.

MADLOMO: You did what?

PROFESSOR: I set your house on fire.

MADLOMO: Do you know what you are saying?

PROFESSOR: There was not only one rapist, there were two of
them.

MADLOMO: You ...?

PROFESSOR: No, not me. My brother, Duma.

MADLOMO: uDuma? The boy who used to drink at my
shebeen; who was always helpful, even to the extent of
getting me sorghum and *umthombo* from the general
dealer store?

PROFESSOR: When the man attacked you, tied you with ropes
and dumped you behind your hut Duma was hiding in
the shadows because he knew you would identify him.
Together they went into the house and raped the baby.

MADLOMO: And you knew all this?

PROFESSOR: I knew of it that night when Duma came back.
He was drunk. We were both drunk and he was
boasting to me that his AIDS would now be cured once
and for all. I panicked. I told him he would go to jail for
a long time if he got caught. I didn't want my brother to
get caught.

MADLOMO: What about my baby, *wena Sathane ndini*?

PROFESSOR: I didn't think about your baby, MaDlomo. I only
thought of my brother. I knew the police would come
and search your house for evidence. Especially the
police from Pietermaritzburg ... those are the ones I
feared most. I had heard of such things as DNA tests

101

and the like. I thought if they came they were sure to discover that Duma had been there as well. So I got petrol, splashed it on your house and set it on fire.

MADLOMO: You wanted to kill my baby to save your brother?

PROFESSOR: I didn't think of the baby. I was not a thinking person at that time. All I wanted was to save Duma.

MADLOMO is dumbstruck. They both sit quietly for a while. THABISILE enters and stares from one to the other.

You'll never know how sorry I am. This has been eating me up for all these years.

MADLOMO: I suppose you feel better now?

PROFESSOR: No, I don't. I feel like a heap of steaming crap.

MADLOMO [*to THABISILE*]: You knew of this?

THABISILE: I learnt of it years later, from his brother, who was dying in a hospital in Durban.

MADLOMO: He has managed to ruin my day. I didn't think anyone could after the sweet taste of victory in court.

An excited SELLER OF LAUGHTER enters, guiding LORD STEWART. SELLER doesn't seem to notice or care that the three people on the stage are standing like statues in different spots, each lost in contemplation.

SELLER: We are going to do it. The Mother of All Jokes! Lord Stewart has agreed that he will be my slave. He says you talked him into it, Professor.

STEWART: I might as well, since I'll be blind forever. They have stopped the blessings. I'll never get to see Our Lady of Benoni.

The SELLER OF LAUGHTER rummages among the flowers and comes up with a plastic bag. He gives it to LORD STEWART.

SELLER: Here, you can have your toast and Simba chip back. I have no need to hold them hostage any more. And it is thanks to you, Professor. Lord Stewart told me he wouldn't be doing it if it were not for you. You are not a bad person after all, Professor. I can even go as far as saying you are a good man, Mr Professor!

STEWART: I've always known he's a good man.

SELLER: Come, Lord Stewart, let's go and prepare for the Mother of All Jokes! I cannot wait to get to the traffic lights with my slave!

They exit.

MADLOMO [*to PROFESSOR*]: I don't think you should have made this confession. You should have just left things as they were. Now I have one more person to hate. You have given me an extra burden of hate to carry with me to my grave.

She exits.

THABISILE: I suppose this is the part where we walk hand-in-hand into the sunset?

PROFESSOR: I hope so. I did what you asked me to do.

THABISILE: I want to be with you, but only after you've paid your debt.

PROFESSOR: You are moving the goalposts.

THABISILE: Go back to KwaVimba and report to the police. Perhaps the magistrate will have mercy on you since you have cracked a case they have long been unable to close. He may give you a very light sentence. I will be waiting for you. Then we can start afresh. In the meantime I will visit you in prison and bring you delicious goodies.

PROFESSOR: You talk of it as if it's a picnic.

THABISILE: We may even remarry while you're serving your sentence, so that you know that when you're done you have someone to come back to.

PROFESSOR: What if I don't go back to KwaVimba to confess my crime? How many people have committed worse crimes and got away with it? Our politicians, for instance?

THABISILE: You are not them. That's why you are here. Anyway, it's up to you. I will never reveal your crime to anyone. And I don't think MaDlomo has any intention of doing anything about it besides carrying the burden of hate. She is not inclined to aggravate the old wounds that you have opened.

PROFESSOR: You forced me to open them.

THABISILE: I didn't force you. I merely said to you that though I want you back I will never be with you because your crime will always stand between us; until you have done the right thing. You said you wanted to be with me.

PROFESSOR: Yes, I want to be with you.

Enter the SELLER OF LAUGHTER leading LORD STEWART, who is in chains. SELLER is carrying a sign with the message: SLAVE MASTER FALLEN ON HARD TIMES. NEEDS MONEY TO FEED SLAVE. He drags LORD STEWART around the stage.

SELLER: Behold, a masterpiece! The Mother of All Jokes. No one can steal this one. They don't have a white man of their own. They will love it at the traffic lights! They will love it! It will stop the traffic!

They exit.

Lights fade to black.

Printed and bound by CPI Group (UK) Ltd, Croydon, CR0 4YY

13/04/2025

14656584-0003